STATE

V.

JACKSON

Third Edition

STATE

V.

JACKSON

Third Edition

Laurence M. Rose

Rebecca Sitterly

Frank D. Rothschild

Based on the original case file *Flinders v. Mismo,*
created by Abraham P. Ordover

NATIONAL INSTITUTE FOR TRIAL ADVOCACY

Reprint Permission
National Institute for Trial Advocacy
361 Centennial Parkway, Suite 220
Louisville, CO 80027
Phone: (800) 225-6482
Fax: (720) 890-7069
E-mail: permissions@nita.org

ISBN 978-1-60156-088-9
FBA 1088

12 11 10   10 9 8 7 6 5 4 3 2

Printed in the United States of America

ACKNOWLEDGMENTS

The authors would like to thank the following people for their assistance in the creation of this case file:

Abraham P. Ordover, Resolution Resources Corporation, Atlanta, Georgia, for his work in writing the original case file, which provides the foundation for this updated version;

Hon. Tommy Jewell, Second Judicial District Court, former Presiding Juvenile Court Judge, Albuquerque, New Mexico, for his portrayal of the banker John Anderson;

Marjorie Martin, Esq., former Assistant District Attorney, Albuquerque, New Mexico, for her portrayal of Sonia Peterson;

Amy Diaz, Esq., Albuquerque, New Mexico, for her portrayal of Marie Williams;

Brad Hall, Esq., Albuquerque, New Mexico, for his portrayal of Arthur Jackson;

R. Thomas Dawe, Esq., Albuquerque, New Mexico, for his portrayal of the examining attorney in the depositions of Marie Williams and John Anderson;

Lieutenant William A. Dunn, Commercial Crimes Bureau, Sheriff Leroy D. Baca, and the men and women of the Los Angeles County Sheriff's Department for their generous provision of fire scene photographs and video clips of High Temperature Accelerant fires, all of which are used in this case file with the express written permission of the Los Angeles County Sheriff's Department;

Senior Criminalists Vickie Clawson and Phil T. Teramoto of the Los Angeles County Sheriff's Department Scientific Services Bureau for their assistance with the Accelerant Analysis Report;

and a very special thanks . . . to Detective Barney Villa, formerly of the Los Angeles County Sheriff's Department, Arson Explosives Unit, for his excellent portrayals of Chief Fire Marshall Olsen and David Pinkus in many NITA Southern California Regional programs over the years, for his invaluable technical expertise, and for his crucial support in gathering people, exhibits, arson scene photographs, and videos for this updated case file.

CONTENTS

CASE SUMMARY

This criminal action was originally brought by the State of Nita against Arthur Jackson and Sonia Peterson. It is claimed that the two arranged for George Avery to destroy the Flinders Aluminum Fabrication Corporation plant on November 16, 2007, by burning the plant. Avery died in the fire. The two defendants were charged with commercial arson.

The case went to trial in 2008 and resulted in a mistrial due to a hung jury, which voted nine to three to convict. Thereafter, Sonia Peterson pled guilty to conspiracy to commit a felony and agreed to testify against Arthur Jackson. The transcripts from the first trial are reproduced here.

Special Instructions

When this case file is used for a full bench or jury trial, the following witnesses may be called:

State

  Marie William

  John Anderson

  Sonia Peterson

  Donald Olsen

Defense

  Janice Jackson

  David Pinkus

  Matthew Korn

  Arthur Jackson (optional)

It has been stipulated that Exhibits 20–23 are business records as defined by section 803(6) and 803(8) of the Federal Rules of Evidence. It has been stipulated that the video clips of the Flinders and Yaphank fires, exhibits 26–27, are actual video footage of those fires.

Suggested Time Limits for Full Trial

Voir Dire	10 minutes per side (5 minutes per attorney when teamed up)
Opening Statement	20 minutes per side
Witness Examination	120 minutes per side
Closing Argument	20 minutes per side

IN THE CIRCUIT COURT OF
DARROW COUNTY, STATE OF NITA
CRIMINAL DIVISION

THE STATE OF NITA,

vs.   CASE NO. CR-70410-1

ARTHUR JACKSON,
SONIA PETERSON
    Defendants.

INFORMATION

Sandra Harris, State Attorney for Darrow County, State of Nita, hereby charges the following offense under the Criminal Code of the State of Nita:

That on November 16, 2007, at 187 River Road, Nita City, Nita, Arthur Jackson and Sonia Peterson committed the crime of Commercial Arson, a violation of Nita Revised Criminal Code Section 672.7, a felony in that they personally or through an agent, did intentionally, willfully, and unlawfully damage by fire or explosion, a building or structure for the purpose of making a false insurance claim that would benefit Arthur Jackson and Sonia Peterson or an entity controlled by, or owned by, Arthur Jackson and/or Sonia Peterson.

Sandra Harris

Sandra Harris
Nita County State Attorny

DATED: March 19, 2008

REVISED CRIMINAL CODE

Section 672.7 Commercial Arson

1. A person commits the crime of commercial arson if he personally or through an agent, intentionally and willfully damages by fire or explosion a building or structure for the purpose of making a false insurance claim that would benefit the person or an entity controlled by, or owned by, the person.

2. Commercial Arson is a felony punishable by confinement in prison for a minimum period of ten years and a maximum period of twenty-five years, a fine of up to $10,000, or both.

Section 842.4 Conspiracy to Commit a Felony

1. A person commits the crime of conspiracy to commit a felony if he agrees with another person to act together to commit an offense that is punishable as a felony, and that either the person or the other commits an act that is pursuant to the plan to commit the felonious offense.

2. Conspiracy to commit a felony is a felony that is punishable by confinement in prison for a period up to ten years, or a fine of $5,000, or both.

TRANSCRIPT OF TESTIMONY
OF MARIE C. WILLIAMS

September 15, 2008

MARIE C. WILLIAMS, called to testify on deposition by the plaintiff and having been duly sworn, testified as follows:

My name is Marie C. Williams. I am thirty-five years old. I live at 2242 169th Avenue, Nita City. I am single with no dependents and live alone. I was employed as a bookkeeper and assistant to the president of the Flinders Aluminum Fabrication Corporation in Nita City.

I was hired as bookkeeper on October 1, 1998. About five years ago, I was also given the title of assistant to the president. I held both positions until August 2007. Thereafter, I held only the bookkeeper post. On December 1, 2007, I was discharged by Mr. Arthur Jackson, the president of the company. I had worked directly for Mr. Jackson since I joined the company. Mr. Jackson and I had a close personal relationship up until August of 2007, when he hired Sonia Peterson as his personal aide. Thereafter, my personal relationship with Mr. Jackson terminated.

He and I had been lovers since 2004. Mr. Jackson is married and has three children, but told me that he was very unhappy and promised that he would leave his wife.

16   Q: Ms. Williams, what did Mr. Jackson say to you about his marriage?

17   A: He said that he was very unhappy at home, and he promised me that he was going to leave his

18   wife. But he never left her, and finally I realized that he had lied to me all along about leaving

19   her.

20   Q: What was your reaction when you realized that?

21   A: I was really, really angry with him, and I finally broke off our relationship that fall when he

22   hired Sonia Peterson.

The company employed from twenty-five to forty workers, depending upon the amount of business it had. The company was administered largely by Mr. Jackson and myself until Ms. Peterson was hired. A separate sales staff was employed. They had little to do with the central administrative functions. We also employed several people in the shipping department.

In 2006, the company had a disastrous year. Losses for the year totaled some $500,000. The year 2007 was even worse. Losses for the first nine months totaled an additional $500,000. Bank loans of $400,000 became due on November 28. In October 2007, Mr. Jackson attempted to renegotiate the loans with the lender, First Trust Bank. I participated in those negotiations with Mr. Jackson and Mr. Anderson, vice president of the bank. The negotiations failed. The loans went unpaid pending receipt of the fire insurance money.

At one meeting with Mr. Anderson, Mr. Jackson spoke of the Avery "designs" and the company's plans to get into the automobile market. Anderson seemed skeptical and requested drawings, market studies, and the like.

At no time were any such studies undertaken by the company. Nor do I recall any negotiations with any automobile manufacturer.

Mr. Anderson also requested that we supply the bank with current financial information. Mr. Jackson never asked me to prepare and send such data to the bank. I don't know if he, Ms. Peterson, or anyone ever sent the information.

On July 14, 2007, Mr. Jackson informed me that if the company didn't pick up new accounts in the last half of the year, it would go under. He complained bitterly of financial problems throughout the months that followed.

Sometime in early September, I overhead a conversation between Mr. Jackson and Ms. Peterson in which she offered to put him in touch with someone named Avery, who, she said, could solve his financial problems. I first saw them sitting and talking by looking through the door to Mr. Jackson's office, which is across from my office. I then walked over to that doorway and, staying out of sight, heard their conversation. With regard to Mr. Avery, I also heard Ms. Peterson describe him as a torch to Mr. Jackson. As best I can recall, the exact words she used were something like: "I know a man named George Avery who can solve all of your financial problems. George is a real torch; he could light up this business for you."

On September 15, 2007, Mr. Avery came to the plant and met with Mr. Jackson. Afterwards, Mr. Jackson asked me to draw a company check to George Avery for $5,000 and give him both the check and one of our spare plant keys. Mr. Jackson told me Mr. Avery was a tool and die designer who would soon be working at the plant to design dies for fabricating parts for use in automobiles. Exhibit 18 is the check I gave to Mr. Avery that day. As I recall, he started working at the plant on October 1.

Also in September, Mr. Jackson contacted the insurance company and increased the fire insurance coverage on the plant, effective October 1. I wrote the check for the increased premium.

I worked late on November 16. I recall that Mr. Jackson came back to the plant at 7:00 p.m. Avery had come in at about 6:30 p.m. One crew was finishing up a rush job. They left at about 6:45 p.m. I was surprised to hear machinery in operation after the last crew had left. I started to go downstairs to check out the matter when I met Mr. Jackson. He was surprised and annoyed to see me there and ordered me to leave at once. I did so. The plant burned down that evening. Avery died in the fire.

1	Q:	When did you see Mr. Jackson next?
2	A:	It was about a day or two after the fire.
3	Q:	What did you say to each other?
4	A:	I told him right off that I suspected that he had paid Avery to burn down the building in order
5		to get the insurance money.
6	Q:	How did he respond?
7	A:	He denied it. He said he didn't do it.
8	Q:	What action did you take based upon your suspicions?
9	A:	I didn't do or say anything right away, but about ten days later, Mr. Jackson fired me. It was
10		after that that I went to the police and talked to Detective O'Brien, and I told him what I
11		suspected Mr. Jackson had done.

It is true that I no longer care for Mr. Jackson, but that is not why I am willing to testify here. I am telling the truth.

Certified by:

Ann E. Hall

Ann E. Hall
Certified Shorthand Reporter (CSR)

Transcript of Testimony
of John Anderson

September 16, 2008

JOHN ANDERSON, called to testify on deposition by the plaintiff and having been sworn, testified as follows:

My name is John Anderson. I am vice president of First Trust Bank in Nita City, and I am in charge of commercial lending for the bank. I graduated from the University of Kansas in 1987 with a business administration degree. I then attended Northwestern University in Chicago and received a master's in business administration in 1991. I received the National Chamber of Commerce Fellowship Grant in my final year and used it to complete a study of innovative ways to finance new business development in urban areas. My area of concentration while in school was studying the reasons for capital flight from urban centers and methods for revitalizing urban business communities.

I moved to Nita City in 1992 after completion of my fellowship and became employed at First Trust Bank as a loan officer in the residential department. I was able to transfer to the commercial department in 1993, as my primary interest is in commercial and business lending. I was a commercial loan officer from 1993 to 1999. At that time the bank reorganized its troubled loan department and established a workout division devoted solely to resolving lending difficulties with companies in default on their commercial loans. I was the manager of that division from its inception to 2002, when I was promoted to the position of vice president in charge of all commercial lending, the position I still hold today.

Flinders Aluminum Company had an outstanding loan that, together with interest, was in the amount of $400,000. Payment of this amount was due November 28, 2007.

During the month of October of that year, I had several meetings with Mr. Arthur Jackson. On one occasion, he was accompanied by an aide, Ms. Marie Williams.

During these meetings, Mr. Jackson sought to refinance the $400,000 loan. His company, he said, was not in a position to make the payment. It had suffered losses of approximately $1,000,000 in the two previous years.

Mr. Jackson informed me of a plan to fabricate auto parts from aluminum for General Motors. He said he had employed a new designer for that purpose and gave me a copy of his resume. He wanted to establish a long-term financing plan for Flinders to accomplish the transition to the new product line.

1	Q:	What information did you ask for, Mr. Anderson?
2	A:	I asked for the current financial data. That included the balance sheet, profit and loss statements,
3		pro forma statements, market analysis. I asked for tax returns.
4	Q:	What information did you request concerning the designs?
5	A:	I wanted to see a design of the product.
6	Q:	What did Mr. Jackson say?
7	A:	Mr. Jackson said that they were working on it and that they would get it into the bank shortly.
8	Q:	What was the discussion about the possibility of additional collateral for the loan?
9	A:	I didn't ask for additional collateral at that time.

I wrote the loan review committee to indicate that we might become an investor in the new venture if it went forward. The bank refused the renegotiation of the existing loan. No current financial information was made available to us by Mr. Jackson.

We took no action on the financing of the new product line. No concrete proposal was ever submitted to us. Nor did we receive the data that we requested.

Certified by:

Ann E. Hall

_____

Ann E. Hall
Certified Shorthand Reporter (CSR)

TRANSCRIPT OF TESTIMONY
OF ARTHUR JACKSON

September 18, 2008

ARTHUR JACKSON, called to testify on deposition by the defendant and having been duly sworn, testified as follows:

My name is Arthur Jackson. I just turned forty, and I am married. My wife, Janice, is thirty-eight years old, and we are currently separated. In the past few years, we have had some problems and disagreements, but it all seemed to come to a head after the fire at the plant. In mid-December 2007, we both agreed that it would be best if I moved out of the family home at 11 Purple Martin Lane, Nita City. I moved into an apartment at 1200 East Gate, Nita City, and I've been living there since. I am the president and sole stockholder of Flinders Aluminum Fabrication Corporation. I purchased the stock of the company in 1996. Prior to my acquisition of Flinders, I was assistant to the president of Cosgrove Aluminum Company for three years. I am a graduate of Nita University and hold an MBA degree from Nita.

The Flinders Corporation was housed in a large, old building. The building, made mostly out of wood and brick, was located at 187 River Road in Nita City. The Flinders building had 50,000 square feet of space, spread out over four floors. The executive offices, including mine and my administrative assistant's, were in the front part of the building on the second floor. While in operation, the company employed between twenty-five and forty workers, depending on the amount of business we had. However, the company has no current operations because of the destruction of its plant.

On November 16, 2007, the company suffered a disastrous fire. On January 3, 2008, Fire Marshal Olsen questioned me and implied that I had started the fire or had Sonia Peterson and/or George Avery do so. They showed me a company check to Avery in the amount of $5,000. George Avery was a designer of tools and dies. I retained his services in September 2007 to assist us in broadening our product line. We had been primarily in the business of fabricating aluminum windows and siding for the home construction market. That market had collapsed. The company had suffered great losses—about $1 million—in the past two years.

19	Q:	Mr. Jackson, how did you first hear about George Avery?
20	A:	George Avery was recommended to me by Sonia, Sonia Peterson, my administrative assistant.
21		She knew of his work from Yaphank and spoke very highly of his designs.
22	Q:	Well, what did you do before hiring him?
23	A:	She discussed his qualifications with me, and then I interviewed him, and after I interviewed
24		him, I retained him.

Avery's office was located on the third floor. He had some splendid suggestions for selling aluminum parts to General Motors for use in place of steel in cars. We were studying that idea in November of 2007.

The idea that Avery was an arsonist is absurd. He was a brilliant designer. His death in the fire was a terrible tragedy. The $5,000 payment to Avery was simply a basic retainer. If his program was successful, he was to receive an additional $100,000.

Fire Marshal Olsen suggested that Avery had burned the Yaphank plant and was implicated in another fire. I know nothing of these matters and find them impossible to believe.

I worked late the evening of November 16, but late hours were not unusual for me; nor, for that matter, were late hours unusual for George Avery.

10	Q:	Who did you talk to before you left that night?
11	A:	I talked with George Avery. It was about 6:45 p.m.
12	Q:	What did he say to you?
13	A:	He said that he was going to work a little longer.
14	Q:	Did you say anything back to him?
15	A:	No, I didn't. That was normal.
16	Q:	Did you see anybody else before you left that night?
17	A:	As a matter of fact, I did. I bumped into Marie Williams.
18	Q:	What time was that?
19	A:	That was closer to seven o'clock.
20	Q:	What did you say to her?
21	A:	Well, she doesn't usually work late, and actually I thought she looked really tired. And I said,
22		"Marie, you look beat. You ought to go home."

Fire Marshal Olsen suggested that I needed money badly. I had no substantial personal needs, but the company did. At one point, I asked my wife for a loan for the business. The company had lost quite a bit of money in the last couple of years. In October of 2007, I told my wife that I needed a loan of at least $100,000. My wife refused to loan the money to me and told me to use my own assets. I told her that my own money was not enough to do the job. I have stocks valued at about $50,000, and my wife and I jointly own our home, which is valued at $150,000. Also, my wife inherited some $300,000 from the estate of her father. That amount has been invested in common stocks of large corporations, including IBM, GM, and General Electric. As of the date of the fire, my wife and I were still together.

Contrary to what the police suggested, I have no women friends. I did have an affair with Marie Williams, but that ended last fall. Marie Williams was my administrative aide for almost five years. However, in August of 2007, I demoted her to her former position of bookkeeper. I then hired Sonia Peterson as my new administrative aide. Ms. Peterson is thirty years old, and she performs her duties quite well. The police, undoubtedly echoing my wife, contended that I was having an affair with Ms. Peterson. This is not true. Ms. Williams was insanely jealous of Ms. Peterson. Her jealousy caused me to end our relationship. Her baseless charges of arson ultimately caused me to discharge her.

My business was really my whole life. Partly because of this, my wife and I quarreled heatedly over the past several months. She claimed I was having a relationship with Sonia Peterson. I denied this, but I knew my wife believed that I was lying. My wife also accused me of being intimate with Marie Williams. Both Marie and I denied that any such relationship existed. My wife and I separated on December 15, 2007. Our separation was largely due to the Peterson business, but there were some financial considerations as well. My wife has custody of our three children: Phyllis, who is twelve; Harry, who is ten; and Ambrose, who is six. I should also note that my wife complained that she was the only one who always had to pay for any extras the family required.

Although Flinders had experienced problems, I felt certain that the business would improve this year. My retention of George Avery shows that I was optimistic at that time. His idea was sound. Auto manufacturers have, in fact, purchased millions of dollars of aluminum parts for replacement of heavier steel parts in their cars. I had every reason to believe this idea would turn the company around.

It would have required a major infusion of new capital into the business to retool. At the time, the company had a loan with First Trust Bank. Payment on the principal and interest in the amount of $400,000 was due November 28, 2007.

In October 2007, I met with John Anderson, vice president of the bank, on several occasions. I sought to refinance the $400,000 loan soon due and to begin consideration of major new financing for the retooling of the plant. Ms. Williams attended at least one of those meetings.

The bank refused to refinance the $400,000 loan, but was prepared to negotiate on the retooling matter once it saw Avery's ideas reduced to working designs. I gave Anderson a copy of Avery's resume. Anderson also demanded that I submit current financials on the company together with market studies and projections covering the new product line.

1   Q: Mr. Jackson, what did you do to meet the bank's requests?

2   A: We were considering what to do at the time of the fire. I needed Avery's designs in order to

3   respond to those requests, and I was planning to contact General Motors with those designs,

4   and other manufacturers. But those designs were lost in the fire.

I was home when I received a phone call about 9:45 p.m. The police told me there was a fire at the plant, and I rushed there only to see the building destroyed.

The authorities investigated the fire and concluded that it was of suspicious origin. They did not, however, arrest me or anyone else. I am aware that Chief Olsen contends that hydrochloric acid was used to start the fire. That material is regularly used in the fabrication process. We always kept five acid-resistant plastic drums on hand, each of which contained ten gallons of the acid. The acid was kept in a storage room on the first floor. No one "started" the fire. I do not know how it started.

The increase in Flinders' fire insurance effective October 1, 2007, was simply a recognition of the effect of inflation. It was normal for me to increase the insurance coverage on the plant from time to time.

Certified by:

Ann E. Hall

Ann E. Hall
Certified Shorthand Reporter (CSR)

Transcript of Testimony
of Janice Jackson

September 18, 2008

JANICE JACKSON, called to testify on deposition by the defendant and having been sworn, testified as follows:

I am Janice Jackson. I am thirty-eight years old. My address is 11 Purple Martin Lane, Nita City. I am separated from Arthur Jackson, who lives at 1200 East Gate. We have three children: Phyllis, twelve; Harry, ten; and Ambrose, six. We separated on December 15, 2007.

I believe that Arthur had an affair with Sonia Peterson. It was not the first time he has had an affair. He had previously been involved with Marie Williams, but he broke off that relationship when I threatened to leave him. I cannot prove he had a relationship with Sonia Peterson, and he denies it. But I don't believe him. He has violated my trust, and we just can't live together anymore. I believe we will get a divorce, but our uncertain financial situation has put that on hold.

Yes, the financial situation before the fire was also precarious. You see, I have my own money, $300,000 that I inherited from my father. It is invested in large companies, such as General Motors and IBM, and is now worth between $750,000 and $1,000,000. I won't touch it since I view it as my children's future. My husband has his own money and stock, and he solely owns his company. All of these items are separate. He gave me money each month to pay for the house, clothing, and groceries. I never really knew how much he made or where his money was kept. He spent it all on the business and probably his girlfriends.

The business was totally separate, and it was his whole life. He loved that business and the people who worked for him. To Arthur, it was a great challenge to stay ahead of the competition and build Flinders into a national firm. He spent more time there than at our house or with me and the children. Yes, we fought over that, too. He always said he was doing it to provide for us, but I told him that he needed to be with the family more. I always paid for vacations with the kids; he was never with us.

I believe that his affair with Marie Williams began in 2004. She was the bookkeeper at the office. It got to a point that I confronted him in August 2007 and threatened to leave him. He vowed to break it off and said it would never happen again. The only reason I stayed with him that long, and stay with him at all now, is for the children. I think that he may have stopped his affair with Marie when Sonia Peterson started at the company. He and Sonia were always "meeting" and talking on the phone. Although I can't prove he had an affair with Sonia, it really didn't matter. In fact, we stopped sleeping in the same room (whenever he was home at all) in December 2007.

In October 2007, around the fourth or fifth, Arthur asked me to loan him $100,000. I told him that there was no way I was going to lend him any of my money. He told me that he was going to the company bank and that a bank loan was due soon, and he wanted to use some money to refinance the loan and pay for some building modifications that he needed to do. I told him to use his own money or get his girlfriend, Sonia, to help. That started a fight, and he left the house.

On November 16, 2007, the night of the fire, Arthur came home at about 7:30 p.m. We had dinner with the children and then watched some television. Arthur told me that he was a little preoccupied that night, because his new design engineer was working late that night on the new product designs. He had talked about this project several times in the months before, and he was really optimistic that his fortune, and our financial picture, would brighten up soon. He was planning to redirect the company into a completely new field and had hired some kind of design guru to help him make this shift. In fact, he said this new man was going to "save his butt." I knew the company had been having a tough time and was happy to see Arthur so enthused about turning things around. At about 9:45 p.m., the phone rang. I answered it. It was the police. They told me that there was a fire at the plant. I told Arthur. He was really shaken. He said that he was going there right away, and he left.

Arthur has not been the best husband or father, but he has never done anything to cause me to believe that he would burn down the business. I'm certain he did no such thing.

Certified by:

Ann E. Hall

_____

Ann E. Hall
Certified Shorthand Reporter (CSR)

TRANSCRIPT OF TESTIMONY
OF SONIA PETERSON

September 19, 2008

SONIA PETERSON, called to testify on deposition by the defendant and having been duly sworn, testified as follows:

I am Sonia Peterson. I live at 88 Charing Cross Muse, Nita City. I was employed by the Flinders company from August 2007 until mid-January 2008. I served as an administrative aide to Mr. Jackson, the president of the company. I am presently unemployed.

I am a single mother with two children: Mark, fourteen, and Brad, eight. Brad is autistic and needs at-home care. I graduated from Nita State University in 1999 with a degree in marketing. Upon graduation I worked at the Firehouse Insurance Company commercial department for one year. I then moved to Yaphank Company where I did marketing with strategic planning for six years until I was let go after a fire. At Yaphank, I oversaw the commercial and industrial storm shutter development.

After Yaphank, I went in with a few partners to begin a consulting business and was the president of the firm. It was called Peterson, Miltown, and Associates and was a venture capital solicitor for start-up companies. Although I wrote excellent business plans for the clients, my partners stole the clients and left me with substantial debts and no medical insurance benefits for my family.

In July 2007, I contacted Arthur Jackson, who I had heard was in financial trouble and looking for a turn-around strategy. I approached Jackson and told him I was interested in helping with strategic decisions and getting in on the ground floor of a solid, industrially based business. He told me that if we were successful, I was going to be shareholder if the company went public. He also told me of some vague concepts about retooling the plant to produce new products, and it was clear that he needed to have a business plan and help for a marketing project. Jackson told me that he wanted to raise some capital to turn the business around but that he didn't want to use the equity in the building and land to recapitalize due to some "community property" issues.

When I arrived at Flinders, I helped draft a business plan, reorganize the files, do a marketing leaflet, and set up PowerPoint presentation packages. I was also told by Jackson to keep the plans from Marie Williams, but I didn't really know why.

I was familiar with the financial problems of the company. It had suffered substantial losses in 2006 and 2007. These losses amounted to almost $1,000,000. Moreover, the company owed $400,000 to First Trust Bank, due November 28, 2007. Mr. Jackson was negotiating with Mr. Anderson of the bank to handle the $400,000 loan and the proposed retooling. Those negotiations were not proceeding well.

I understand that Anderson wanted projections and market studies done in connection with the retooling. We lacked the expertise to do such studies. I assumed we would hire an independent expert to prepare this data. We hadn't gotten that far when the fire put an end to the plans.

I was never asked to, nor did I, send any financial information to the bank.

Mr. Jackson was seeking methods of turning the company around. He believed that the company needed to develop new product lines in order to survive. One idea that he had was the fabrication of auto parts from aluminum rather than steel. Other companies were making substantial fortunes in that line.

In September or October 2007, I recommended George Avery, a tool and die designer, to Mr. Jackson. Avery had been hired by my former employer, the Yaphank Company, and he had done excellent design work for them. He also did work for Fass Meatpacking. The Yaphank plant did burn down shortly after Avery was hired, but certainly he had nothing to do with that. After all, Yaphank was rebuilt.

1 Q: Ms. Peterson, what did you do to check on Avery's background?

2 A: Well, I didn't check on his credentials, but I was familiar with his background. I knew that he

3   was an independent type. He liked to work as an independent contractor and move around a

4   lot. In addition to working as a tool and die designer for the Yaphank Company and Fass

5   Meatpacking, he also worked for General Dynamics and McDonnell Douglas and American

6   Motors Company.

7 Q: What else did you know about his background?

8 A: Well, I knew that he was a graduate engineer and that he'd attended Cornell and MIT.

9 Q: How do you know that?

10 A: Well, I never checked on his degrees. I didn't call the schools, but I do remember that from his

11   resume.

12 Q: Do you know whether Mr. Jackson checked?

13 A: I do not know. I never talked to Mr. Jackson as to whether he checked on Mr. Avery's

14   credentials.

As I understand it, there are some wild assertions that I was having an affair with Mr. Jackson. Actually, I find him a good man, but unattractive.

I also have been told that Ms. Williams says I described Mr. Avery as a "torch." Ms. Williams is mistaken.

Certified by:

Ann E. Hall

Ann E. Hall
Certified Shorthand Reporter (CSR)

TRANSCRIPT OF TESTIMONY
OF MATTHEW KORN

September 19, 2008

MATTHEW KORN, called to testify on deposition by the plaintiff and having been duly sworn, testified as follows:

My name is Matthew Korn. I am president of Yaphank Company, which manufactures metal storm shutters.

In June 2006, I became acquainted with George Avery, who applied to our company for a position as a tool and die designer. I interviewed him, and he presented himself well. I was interested in his experience in connection with a new process I was thinking of developing; it was a crimping process to make our shutter edges more user friendly. I checked out Avery's references at McDonnell Douglas, General Dynamics, and Ross Metal. They described him as a loner but very talented. I tried to check out his academic references at Cornell and MIT, which were listed on his resume, but could not confirm them. The people I spoke with said that there was no record of his attendance under that name. But that didn't really matter to me, as his work references were excellent.

Shortly after Avery began his work, we suffered a disastrous fire in our plant. In fact we were closed for a period of time and laid off most of our employees, including Avery. I do know that Avery moved to the Fass plant to work, and I used him for two to three months as a part-time consultant after we rebuilt the plant with the insurance proceeds.

Sonia Peterson worked for me from 2000 to 2006, but we had to let her go after the fire. She was a good marketing manager. I did not know her well, but only in connection with the business. I do know that she knew Avery while he was with us, as their offices were near each other and they came together to the office cookout in June.

I also am familiar with Chief Olsen. After our fire, he made lots of noise regarding the fire, claiming it was arson. Nothing ever came from his noise, and I told him to either bring me up on charges or shut up. It was only after I threatened to sue him that he stopped talking about our fire.

It is true that our company was having certain financial problems before the fire and that we used hydrochloric acid in large amounts as part of our manufacturing process. I don't see what that's got to do with anything.

Certified by:

Ann E. Hall

Ann E. Hall
Certified Shorthand Reporter (CSR)

IN THE CIRCUIT COURT OF
DARROW COUNTY, STATE OF NITA
CRIMINAL DIVISION

THE STATE OF NITA,

vs.   CASE NO. CR-70410-1

ARTHUR JACKSON,
SONIA PETERSON
    Defendants.

PLEA AGREEMENT

COMES NOW, Sandra Harris, State Attorney of Nita City, Nita, by and through the undersigned Assistant State Attorney and hereby enters into this contract for a plea agreement with the defendant, Sonia Peterson.

The terms of the agreement are as follows:

1. The defendant shall plead guilty to one (1) count of conspiracy as charged in the amended information filed in this cause. The Court shall adjudicate the defendant guilty and sentence the defendant to three years of probation. The defendant's plea of guilty shall be irrevocable.

2. In addition to all of the standard conditions of probation, the following special conditions of probation are made part of the defendant's sentence and the defendant expressly agrees to these special conditions of probation.

    a. The defendant agrees to be debriefed by any local, state, or federal law enforcement agents at the direction of the State Attorney with regards to her knowledge of, or participation in, any criminal activity occurring inside and outside of Nita City, Nita.

    b. The defendant agrees to give complete and truthful information in any such debriefings and specifically agrees not to falsely implicate any person.

    c. The defendant agrees to testify at any statements, depositions, or before any court or grand jury when called upon to do by the State Attorney, the court, or any other party with an interest in the litigation.

    d. The defendant agrees to act as a protective source in undercover investigations at the direction of the State Attorney.

Defendant's Initial ___

3. The defendant must not claim any privilege or Fifth Amendment right to remain silent when questioned about the circumstances of the instant case or any other criminal acts of which she has knowledge.

4. The parties agree that this agreement provides immunity from prosecution of the defendant for her direct or indirect involvement as a principal in the crime charged in the initial information.

5. The defendant agrees to submit to polygraph examinations at the direction of the State Attorney to determine the truthfulness of any statements or testimony provided pursuant to this Agreement and further agrees that the results of such examination shall be admissible against her in any probation violation hearing that may result. The State Attorney agrees that the defendant cannot be precluded from introducing evidence of compliance at any such hearing.

6. All of the agreements between the State of Nita and the defendant are contained within this plea agreement. There are no other agreements between the Office of the State Attorney and the defendant.

Wherefore, the State of Nita and the defendant do hereby move this Honorable Court to accept and ratify this Plea Agreement, after taking the appropriate plea colloquy and meeting all other requirements for the acceptance of a plea.

This agreement being entered into on the **10th day** of **December 2008**, in Nita City, Nita.

So agreed,

State Attorney

_____
By:
Assistant State Attorney

_____
Sonia Peterson
Defendent

_____
Attorney for Defendant

Defendant's Initial _____

Notes of Interview: Sonia Peterson

By State Attorney
December 10, 2008

Ms. Peterson admitted that she and Jackson conspired to burn down the Flinders building. One night in early September 2007, after a particularly late working night, Arthur grabbed her and kissed her. She really needed the job, so she really didn't protest. They ended up having sexual relations that night at the office. According to Peterson that was the only such occurrence in their relationship. Thereafter, she always made excuses to make sure that she would never be "available" if he made another pass. She is not happy to talk about that night's event, and she also knows that Jackson will deny the occurrence of that evening.

The night that she and Arthur were together, she made an offhand remark that they would work together to have Flinders rise from the ashes "like a phoenix." Arthur responded by saying he "would like to make the place ashes." The next day at the office, she told him that she knew a man named Avery whom she had dated and worked with at Yaphank, and who had told her that he had burned down the Yaphank plant for money. Then she told him that she would introduce him to Avery. Arthur said to her, "Now that is strategic planning, and if it all works, there will be a bonus in it for you."

She introduced Avery to Jackson in the next week in mid-September and urged Jackson to appear to be pursuing the possible bank financing with First Bank. She suggested that these bank discussions would provide an alibi when the fire occurred. After the fire, she was to get half of Avery's "separation compensation" of $100,000.

On the night of the fire, Jackson and Avery told her to stay home with her children. After the fire, when she heard that Avery had died, she was afraid that she might be discovered due to her previous relationship with Avery. She talked with Jackson about Avery's death. Jackson told her to "keep your mouth shut and this will all go away." She said she followed his directions through the first trial, but when the verdict was hung she began to worry about her children.

Exhibit 1

Mismo Fire Insurance Policy

The Mismo Fire Insurance Company

FIRE INSURANCE POLICY
No. 951946

AGREEMENT between the Mismo Fire Insurance Company (hereinafter the "Company") and the Flinders Aluminum Fabrication Corporation (hereinafter the "Insured").

The policy is to take effect January 1, 1998.

FACE AMOUNT: $835,000.

INSURED PREMISES: The plant and property of the insured located at 187 River Road, Nita City, Nita 99997

ENDORSEMENTS:

Face amount: Increased to $1,125,000, January 1, 2003.

Face amount: Increased to $1,667,000, October 1, 2007.

[The standard fire insurance policy is omitted. Clause 9 of that policy states as follows:]

9.   ARSON: The Company shall not be liable for loss caused by or resulting from arson where the same was occasioned by the deliberate acts of the insured or any agents thereof.

Exhibit 2

Olsen Field Report

CITY OF NITA
BUREAU OF FIRE INVESTIGATION

FIELD REPORT

Inv. __Flinders Aluminum__   Date of Inv.   __11/16 and 11/17/2007__

Time of Alarm __8:30 p.m.__   Date of Alarm __11/16/ 2007__

Fire Location __187 River Road, Nita City__

Type of Building __Ind. Plant; wood, brick; circa 1914__

Cause of Fire __Hydrochloric acid intentionally released and encountering an open flame.__

Fire Department __Nita__

Occupant __Flinders Aluminum__

         Address __same__

Owner __Arthur Jackson__

  Address __11 Purple Martin Lane, Nita City__

Arrests _____

Deaths __(1) male; cauc.__   Closed _____   Open XX

Arson Detective __Olsen__   Police at Scene: Yes __XX__ No _____

Preliminary Classification __Incendiary__

Remarks: HCL stored in large quantities on the premises was used to cause the explosion and fire. The localized destruction and eyewitness accounts of the rapid horizontal spread of the fire support this classification. Obtained video footage of fire from local news channel. Photographs of deceased taken after fire extinguished. This investigator at scene beginning 6:00 a.m. 11/17. Photographs of scene and location of deceased obtained 11/17. Suggest file remain open for further investigation.

Donald Olsen

Date: 11/17/2007
Form BFI 202   Investigator: Donald Olsen, Chief

Exhibit 3

Olsen Report of Supplemental Investigation

CITY OF NITA

BUREAU OF FIRE INVESTIGATION

REPORT OF SUPPLEMENTAL INVESTIGATION

Re: Flinders Aluminum Fabrication Corp., 187 River Rd, Nita City

Reference: Field Report, BFI 202, 11/17/2007

The deceased found on the premises has been identified as one George Avery, 57, of 2318 Crescent Street, Nita City.

Cause of death, as established by medical examiner, was from multiple injuries sustained in the explosion.

Avery has been investigated previously by this office in connection with fires at the Yaphank Co. and Fass Meatpacking Co.

This investigator conducted both investigations at the time of the fires, and I have reviewed the videotape footage of the Yaphank fire, which I had obtained from a local news channel and stored in the archives of our offices. The video footage of the Flinders fire compared to the video footage of the Yaphank fire indicates similarities in flame color, smoke color, and flame reaction to water. Avery had been employed by Yaphank as a designer of metal fittings. The fire occurred two weeks after his initial employment. Although the Yaphank fire was likely arson, there was insufficient evidence upon which to base an arrest.

The Yaphank plant was rebuilt following the fire. Avery was re-employed by them on a part-time basis for several months.

The Fass fire was also likely caused by arson. Mr. Avery was a paid consultant to Fass. He was retained by them six weeks prior to the fire. The Fass fire was caused by the explosion of HC1, apparently ignited by a mixture of calcium hydrochloride with a common hair shampoo. Oxidation within minutes caused a hot fire, which likely ignited the HC1. The company went out of business following the fire.

This could have been the setup at Flinders. The traces of the igniter in this case were likely washed away by the fire hoses. However, it appears that one of the machines in the shop had been operating just prior to the fire. HC1 combining with hot metal can create an explosive situation.

Donald Olsen

—————————————————————
Investigator: Donald Olsen, Chief

Date: 11/27/2007
Form BFI 204

Exhibit 4

Olsen Bureau Report

CITY OF NITA

BUREAU OF FIRE INVESTIGATION

REPORT

TO: Detective O'Brien, Nita City Police Department

FROM: Chief Fire Marshal Olsen
Bureau of Fire Investigation

DATE: December 18, 2007

SUBJECT: Report of fire occurring on the night of November 16, 2007, at an industrial plant located at 187 River Road, Nita City, owned by Flinders Aluminum Corporation.

BUILDING DESCRIPTION

The fire occurred at an industrial plant. The building was four stories high, constructed of wood and brick, approximately 50,000 square feet overall and built in 1915. The building contained an inventory of aluminum products.

DESCRIPTION OF FIRE

The fire occurred on November 16, 2007, at approximately 8:00 p.m. The fire was discovered by Alison Smith, who was passing by the plant on the way home from visiting a friend. Ms. Smith contacted the Nita City Fire Department at 8:30 p.m. Four units responded to the fire and arrived at the scene at 8:36 p.m.

The fire was of considerable size at the time the first fire trucks arrived at the scene. The smoke was reddish brown and was accompanied by large flames. The fire was large and spreading in a horizontal direction at a rapid speed. It took five hours, an unusually long time, to bring the fire under control. The flames became brighter and changed color when hit with a stream of water from a hose. An inspection of the debris indicated that there was one independent origin of the fire.

DAMAGE

The building was almost entirely destroyed. Only one section of the northwest wall of the building was left standing. The fire caused one fatality. This individual was identified as George Avery, a white male, approximately 57 years old.

ADDITIONAL FINDINGS

A chemical analysis of the ashes revealed the presence of hydrochloric acid (HCl). An examination of the remaining structure showed that the windows either had been open or were blown out.

My investigation ruled out the usual accidental causes per the NFPA 921 Guide for Fire and Explosion Investigations. Accidental fires involve those for which the proven cause does not involve an intentional human act to ignite or spread the fire. The point of origin was a large combination storeroom and machine shop on the first floor of the building. Analysis of the debris, burn patterns, and damage indicated a "hot spot" in that location and that an explosion had taken place.

I have inspected these premises many times in the course of fire prevention duties. No faulty electrical wiring or motors were found. No heating devices were located near the point of origin. Machines used in coating the aluminum were in the area and apparently had been in use up until shortly before the fire. These machines were equipped with timer starting devices and were capable of being preset to operate automatically.

Hydrochloric acid is not flammable in and of itself. However, under certain conditions it is highly explosive. These conditions would have to have been intentionally created for ignition of the instant fire.

The proper storage of hydrochloric acid is imperative. Many materials provide unsuitable containers because hydrochloric acid is so highly corrosive. The choice of container is dependent upon the quantity of acid to be stored. When a large quantity of hydrochloric acid (such as 10,000 gallons) is to be stored, then the proper container would be a plastic or rubber-lined steel tank. This combination would have the structural strength of steel and the nonreactive nature of rubber or plastic. When a smaller quantity of hydrochloric acid (such as 50 gallons) is stored, a plastic drum is recommended. Because hydrochloric acid may contain traces of hydrofluoric acid, which attacks fiberglass, as a safety measure a container of fiberglass lined with plastic is not recommended.

When a plastic container or liner is used for storage, the hydrochloric acid cannot compromise the integrity of the plastic and leak out of the container. This is because plastic is chemically inert to the acid. Glass could also be used, but problems arise with the tendency for glass to break and the difficulty of repair. An acid leak would occur if the container was ruptured (by a forklift, for instance), if the container was faulty, if the container was sabotaged, or if the wrong drum was used.

Serious problems may arise if hydrochloric acid is improperly stored and leaks out of its container. If the acid contacts a ferrous metal, such as steel, then hydrogen is generated. Hydrogen is an explosive gas. The chemical formula of this reaction is

$$2HCl + Fe \rightarrow FeCl_2 + H_2$$

$$\text{(L)} \quad \text{(S)} \qquad \text{(S)} \qquad \text{(G)}$$

$$\text{(L) = liquid; (S) = solid; (G) = gas}$$

Whereas hydrochloric acid is not in itself explosive, if it contacts steel it will release hydrogen. If the hydrogen encounters an ignition source, an explosion would occur.

CAUSE OF FIRE

The reddish brown color of the smoke, together with the large flames, indicates that substances containing nitrocellulose fiber, sulfur, or sulfuric, nitric, or hydrochloric acid were burning. The fact that flames burned brighter and changed color when hit with water is another indication that an accelerant was used. Difficulty in extinguishing the fire also points to the use of an accelerant. A chemical analysis of the ashes showed that hydrochloric acid, an explosive substance when combined with hot metal, in fact was burning. When HCl comes in contact with ferrous metals, hydrogen is released, and when hydrogen is combined with air, it may cause an explosive situation. Although hydrochloric acid is normally present in the plant, scarring of the concrete floor plus chemical analysis showed that an unusually large amount was located at the point of origin of the fire. Moreover, the magnitude of the fire and its rapid spreading indicate that several hundred gallons of the acid likely were splashed about the source of the fire. Normally, a plant of this type and size would maintain a supply of approximately fifty gallons of hydrochloric acid for cleaning purposes. This would likely be stored in one place. Analysis of the debris indicates an explosion at the point of origin, likely caused by a time release igniter, possibly the preset timer of one of the machines or calcium hydrochloride mixed with shampoo.

The large flames are an indication that the fire was well ventilated. Favorable ventilation conditions were created by the explosion in order to ensure that the ensuing fire spread quickly. Such unusually good ventilation would not normally be present since the building is enclosed and the windows would be shut on a November evening. Lack of ventilation would be necessary for the explosion. That, in turn, would create the ventilation needed for the fire to spread. A professional would know how to blow out the windows. Another factor pointing to deliberate ignition is the rapid progress made by the fire. According to Ms. Smith, from 8:30 p.m., when she first discovered the fire, to 8:36 p.m., when the first fire trucks arrived at the scene, the fire had spread tremendously.

Field Investigator Henderson, who was present at the scene of the blaze, reported that the flames spread quickly in a horizontal direction. This is another indication that good ventilation existed. Fire sweeps upward until it is blocked by some obstruction. When the fire is blocked, it travels through any available crack or opening. If there are no openings, the flames spread horizontally until the fire can sweep around the obstruction. When good ventilation conditions do not exist, the horizontal spread is slow. The fact that the horizontal travel of the fire was rapid indicated that favorable ventilation existed.

George Avery, whose body was found in the debris of the machine shop, died of multiple injuries resulting from the explosions. The autopsy report indicates that the fatal injury was to the chest. Field Investigator Henderson also obtained photographs of Avery's body at the scene, as well as photographs of the location of the body marked by outline tape the following morning. FI Henderson also took photographs of the plant debris and remaining wall section after the fire was extinguished.

We had previously come into contact with Avery in connection with other investigations. Our normal practice in an arson case is to investigate all persons connected with the enterprise and, without exception, an investigation of any corpse found on the premises would be made.

Our investigation of Avery showed that he had been linked to two other fires that were of incendiary origin. One fire destroyed a factory owned by the Yaphank Company. Mr. Avery had been employed by Yaphank for only two weeks prior to the fire. The other fire destroyed a warehouse at the Fass Meatpacking Company. Although these fires were likely the result of arson, there was insufficient evidence for an arrest. Mr. Avery, who was associated with these businesses when the fires occurred, was questioned on both occasions. This marshal conducted both investigations. In connection with this investigation, I reviewed Avery's resume, which I obtained from John Anderson at First Trust Bank. I checked with Cornell and MIT, schools from which Avery indicated on his resume he had graduated. Neither had any record of George Avery.

Contrary to popular belief, a substantial number of arsonists are trapped and killed in their own fires. For the most part, these persons are less than skilled at the techniques of arson. It is less likely that a professional arsonist would be caught in his own fire, but not particularly unusual.

CONCLUSION

This marshal concludes that the fire was the result of arson. This conclusion is based upon the following factors:

1. The unusually large amount of hydrochloric acid that was located at the point of origin of the fire and apparently splashed about the room. Hydrogen likely was released and, in combination with ferrous metal, exploded by some sort of time release device that malfunctioned.

2. The unusually rapid spread of the fire, caused by favorable ventilation conditions not normally present.

3. The presence of George Avery in the building at the time of the fire.

Submitted by:

Donald Olsen

_____

Donald Olsen
Chief Fire Marshal

EXHIBIT 5

Olsen Memorandum

TO: File   *DO*

FROM: Chief Olsen

DATE: January 3, 2008

RE: Flinders Company Fire, 11/16/2007

I interviewed Arthur Jackson, president of Flinders Aluminum Fabrication Corp., at his home on January 3, 2008. Jackson denied the arson. He admitted that Peterson had introduced him to Avery, the alleged designer. He seemed surprised (he said) by my assertion that Avery was a torch. I told him of Avery's work at the Yaphank Co. and that the Yaphank plant had burned down. He identified Avery as the man he hired to do design work, but denied knowledge of any fire at Yaphank. He reacted the same way when I told him of Avery's connection with the Fass Co., which also suffered a terrible fire.

He admitted paying Avery $5,000.

He admitted that HCl was kept at the plant in quantities of about fifty gallons.

I asked him if he personally checked on Avery's credentials listed on his resume or any references Avery may have supplied. He said he left such matters to Ms. Peterson.

He said he had no motive because his wife had assets of around $300,000 and he had personal assets of about $50,000.

On the evening of the fire, he visited the plant to pick up some papers from his office. This was at about 7:00 p.m. He left the plant by 7:30 p.m.

He said he dismissed Marie Williams from her position because she was becoming a pest and an embarrassment. He admitted that they had been lovers and asked if this information could be kept confidential.

EXHIBIT 6

Olsen Resume

RESUME OF DONALD OLSEN

BIOGRAPHICAL

Born in Nita City, Nita in 1950. Married to Rita Olsen, two children.

EDUCATIONAL BACKGROUND

Graduated from Darrow High School in Nita City in 1968. Attended classes at Lincoln Community College in general curriculum from 1968 to 1970. Enlisted in United States Army in 1970 and served in Fort Sill, Oklahoma and Weisenstadt, Germany APO until 1975.

Attended Nita Fire Department Training School in East Meadow, Nita in 1976, including basic courses in fire investigation and fire fighting.

Completed additional six-month arson investigation course at Nita Fire Department Training School and received certification by state and national training review agencies.

WORK HISTORY

1977 to 1982	Fireman, East Meadow Fire Department, East Meadow, Nita; arson investigator for two years
1982 to 1992	Marshal, Arson Bureau, East Meadow Fire Department, Nita
1992 to 1997	Chief, Arson Bureau, East Meadow Fire Department, Nita
1997 to present	Chief, Nita Fire Department Bureau of Fire Investigation

Exhibit 7

Flinders Floor Plan (1st floor)

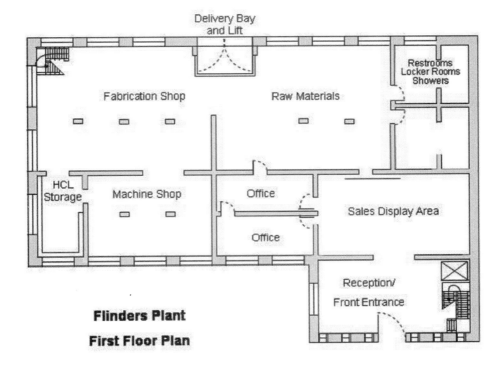

Flinders Plant

First Floor Plan

EXHIBIT 8

Flinders Floor Plan (2nd floor)

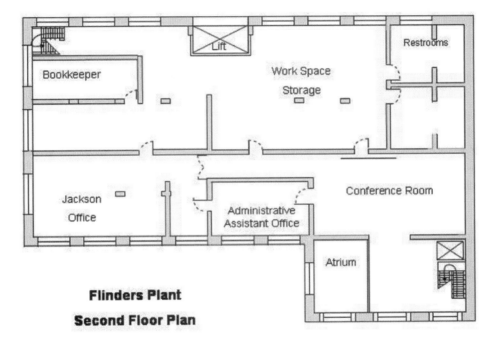

Flinders Plant

Second Floor Plan

EXHIBIT 9

Flinders Floor Plan (3rd floor)

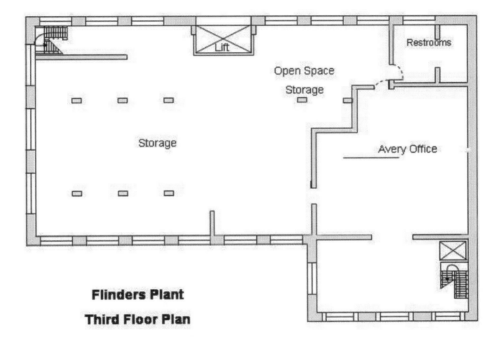

Exhibit 10

Flinders Floor Plan (4th floor)

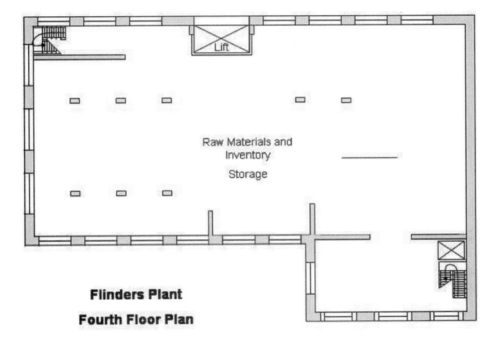

Flinders Plant

Fourth Floor Plan

EXHIBIT 11

Photograph of Flinders
Pre-Fire

EXHIBIT 12

Photograph of Flinders
Post-Fire

EXHIBIT 13

Photograph of Fass Meatpacking Company

EXHIBIT 14

Photograph of Yaphank Company

EXHIBIT 15

George Avery Resume

GEORGE A. AVERY	2318 Crescent Street, Nita City	Phone (620) 980-6845 E-mail avery@mindspring.net

Education	1969 to 1973	Cornell University, Bachelor of Science in Engineering, Graduated cum laude
	• 1973	Science Prize from University Board of Trustees
	1973 to 1975	Massachusetts Institute of Technology, MA Industrial Engineering Master's Thesis: "Metallurgical Processes in Industrial Grade Steel Fastener Failures"
Professional experience	• 1975 to 1978	Crown Engineering, Intern, Draftsman
	• 1978 to 1979	Crown Engineering, Journeyman Draftsman
	• 1980 to 1982	Ross Metal Industries, Senior Draftsman
	• 1982 to 1985	Ross Metal Industries, Design Protocol
	• 1986 to 1987	Chevrolet Trucks, Senior Draftsman
	• 1988 to 1989	BMI, Senior Draftsman
	• 1990 to 1991	General Dynamics, Senior Draftsman
	• 1992 to 1993	McDonald Douglas, Engine Tool and Die Unit
	• 1993 to 1995	McDonald Douglas, Design Protocol Division
	• 1996 to 1997	Ford Motor Company Parts Integration
	• 1998 to 1999	General Dynamics, Engine Parts Testing and Design
	• 2000 to 2001	Ford Motor Company Parts Integration
	• 2002 to 2003	Macauley Equipment Manufacturing, Tool and Die Design
	• 2004 to 2005	Yaphank Company, Metal Fittings Design
	• 2006	Fass Meatpacking Company, Tool and Die Design Consultant
Patents and publications	1992	Patent Application for Manifest Coupler U.S. Patent No. A78-3847659328
References	Suzanne Barker, Chevrolet Trucks, (760) 474-7285	
	Henry Arnett, Ross Metal Industries, (630) 243-0956	
	Jack Darnell, General Dynamics Corporation, (890) 583-3487	

Exhibit 16

George Avery Photograph

EXHIBIT 17

Photograph of Avery Body Outline

Exhibit 18

Avery Check

Flinders Aluminum Fabricating Corp.	136
187 River Road	71-74242712
Nita City, Nita 99990	

Date **September 15, 2007**

Pay to
the Order of **George Avery** $ **5 000.00**

Five Thousand & °°/100   *Dollars*

FIRST TRUST BANK   *Flinders Aluminum Fabricating Corp.*
Nita City, Nita 99990

271274241:   13 628   000500000

EXHIBIT 19

Autopsy Report

STATE OF NITA
COUNTY OF DARROW

Office of Medical Examiner
(721) 555-3200

County/City Building
Nita City, Nita 99990

AUTOPSY REPORT
George Avery

Information available at time of autopsy

This fifty-seven-year-old Caucasian male was found beneath the debris of an explosion at a local aluminum plant.

Under the provisions of Nita Code 21-205, a postmortem examination including autopsy of the body is performed in the Darrow County Medical Examiner's Office on November 17, 2007, commencing at 10:00 a.m.

External examination of the body

The decedent is brought to the morgue in a disaster bag. Clothing includes a blue plaid, long-sleeve shirt on which the sleeves are burned and the seams on the sleeves are torn, a pair of blue jeans that have numerous types of particulate debris on them, a pair of white briefs, a pair of white crew socks, and a pair of white Nike tennis shoes. These items of clothing are forwarded to the Crime Laboratory.

This is the unembalmed body of a white male that weighs 175 pounds and measures six feet in height. The stature is mesomorphic, rigor mortis is generalized, and lividity is dorsal and not fixed and has a pinkish discoloration. No other decompositional changes are noted, and the overall appearance of the body is that of a well-developed white male, consistent with the stated age of fifty-seven years. The hair is light brown, of medium length, and shows frontal parietal balding. Portions of the hair in the frontal region have been scorched. The external auditory meati are unremarkable. The irises are blue, and the pupils are equally dilated. The nasal and oral cavities contain a small amount of bloody froth. The teeth are the decedent's natural teeth and are in average condition. There are first- and second-degree burns over the skin of the face and cheeks, and there is a 1½-inch angulated laceration over the ramus of the right mandible, which is a full thickness laceration and appears to represent some impact with an object that has a right angle on its surface.

The neck is unremarkable.

The upper extremities are remarkable in that there are first- and second-degree burns over the skin of the hands and distal forearms and there is a compound fracture of the right humerus.

The torso is remarkable in that there are numerous fractures of the ribs bilaterally, which can be palpated through the skin. There are three small ecchymoses over the left pectoral region, and there are numerous superficial scrapes over the skin of the lumbar region. On the back there is a three inch in diameter circular contusion, which is definitely patterned and is essentially a series of ½-inch arcs that form a "broken circle." It is located over the right scapula.

The external genitalia are those of a normal adult male; the penis is circumcised, and both testes are descended.

The lower extremities are remarkable only in that there are several ecchymoses over the anterior surfaces of both tibias that are of various ages and there are several acute contusions over the right patella.

Internal examination of the body

Head

The skin of the scalp is retracted in the usual manner, and there are several areas of soft tissue hemorrhage in the scalp over the right and left frontal parietal regions.

The underlying calvarium is intact, and upon its removal there is no blood in the epidural, subdural, or subarachnoid space. The cerebral gyri are moderately broadened and flattened, and the sulci are moderately obliterated. Coronal sectioning of this 1250-gram brain demonstrates no gross abnormalities other than cerebral edema. There is no herniation. The dura is reflected from the base of the skull, and there is no evidence of basilar skull trauma.

Chest and Abdomen

The skin of the chest and abdomen is opened with the usual "Y"-shaped incision, which demonstrates a ½-inch layer of yellow subcutaneous adipose tissue. There is moderate amount of hemorrhage in the subcutaneous fat over the chest and abdomen. Upon reflection of the skin flaps, the right ribs two through six can be palpated to be fractured in the axillary line and the left ribs two through seven have been fractured in the anterior axillary line.

Upon removal of the chest plate, there is a bilateral hemothorax totaling two liters. The rib fractures have penetrated the parietal pleura and have caused bilateral pulmonary contusions and lacerations. Both lungs are collapsed.

The skin of the neck is dissected up to the angle of the jaw, and there is no evidence of soft tissue trauma to the major airways or vital surrounding structure of the lateral neck compartments.

The thoracic and abdominal organs are examined in situ, then removed by the Virchow technique for serial examination.

Major Airways

The larynx, trachea, and major bronchi are unremarkable except that there is a small amount of blood adherent to the mucosa and there is a moderate amount of soot in the airways.

Lungs

The right lung weighs 500 grams, and the left lung 460 grams. Both lungs are collapsed and atelectatic. There are bilateral pulmonary contusions, and there is mild anthracotic change on the pleural surfaces. There are no mass lesions seen on serial sectioning of the lungs. There are focal areas of parenchymal hemorrhage surrounding the pulmonary contusions, and the pulmonary veins have been lacerated bilaterally at the hila.

Heart

The heart weighs 290 grams. There is concentric left ventricle hypertrophy. The epicardium, endocardium, valve leaflets, and chordae tendineae are unremarkable. The coronary arteries show mild atherosclerotic plaquing, but the degree of occlusion is not significant.

Gastrointestinal Tract

The esophagus is unremarkable. The stomach contains two cups of partially digested food, which consists primarily of noodles with a small amount of slightly chewed meat, which appears to be beef. The small bowel, large bowel, appendix, and rectum are unremarkable.

Hepatobiliary System

The liver weighs 1900 grams and is congested. The gall bladder contains fifteen cc's of watery green bile and no stones. The extrahepatic biliary ducts are patent.

Spleen

The spleen weighs 120 grams, has a wrinkled capsule, and has a small laceration near the posterior pole of the hilum. There are about 150 cc's of blood in the splenic bed.

Pancreas

The pancreas weighs 110 grams, has a coarsely lobulated appearance, and soft consistency on cross section.

Urinary System

The right kidney weighs 140 grams, and the left kidney 150 grams. Both capsules strip easily from the cortical surfaces, and the kidneys have the typical cortex and dark medulla consistent with "shock kidney." The ureters are unremarkable, and the bladder mucosa is within normal limits. The bladder contains about 150 cc's of dilute urine.

Endocrines

The thyroid and adrenals are unremarkable. The parathyroids are not identified.

Great Vessels

The great vessels of the thorax and abdomen and the tributaries thereof are unremarkable except for acute trauma to the pulmonary veins noted above.

Other procedures

1. Blood and urine are submitted for toxicology.
2. Documentary photographs are taken.
3. Clothing is submitted to the Crime Laboratory for accelerant analysis.
4. Autopsy diagrams marked with location of injuries.

Gross diagnoses

1. First- and second-degree burns to face and distal forearms and hands.
2. Bilateral rib fractures and bilateral pneumothorax and hemothorax.
3. Bilateral pulmonary contusions with lacerations of pulmonary vein.
4. Fracture of right humerus.
5. Laceration of spleen.
6. Patterned contusion, back.
7. Patterned laceration, skin over right mandible.

Causes of death

BLUNT TRAUMA, PRIMARILY TO CHEST causing victim to hemorrhage into chest cavity. Combination of trauma from blow and blood in chest cavity resulted in collapse of lungs and inability to breathe.

Ronald Harrison

Ronald Harrison, M.D.
Medical Examiner
RH:sd

DATE: November 18, 2007

EXHIBIT 20

Autopsy Diagram (front-rear)

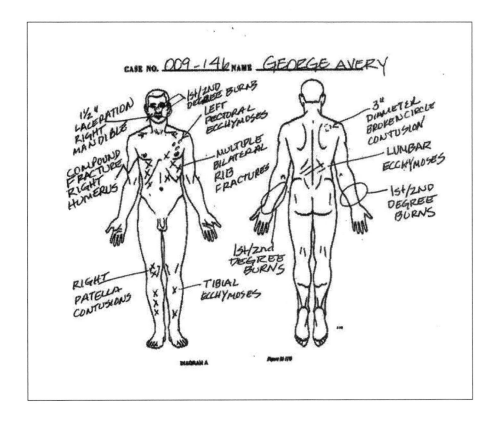

Exhibit 21

Autopsy Diagram (hand)

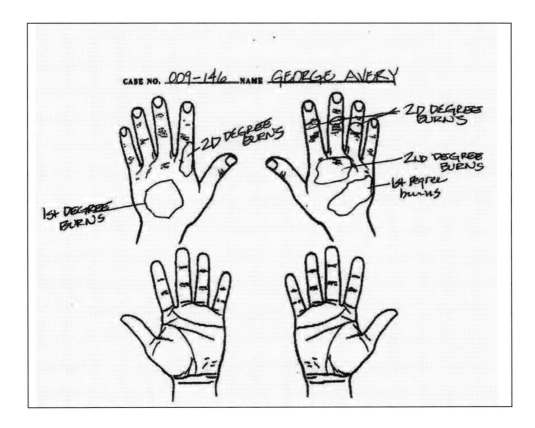

Exhibit 22

Autopsy Diagram (side)

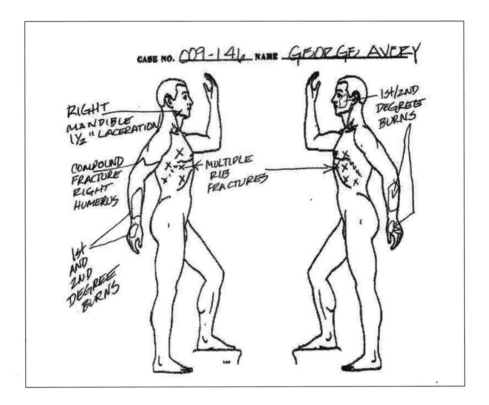

Exhibit 23

Accelerant Analysis Report

CITY OF NITA - POLICE DEPARTMENT

Crime Laboratory	Accelerant Analysis Report

Physical Evidence Section 232 Barnett Nita City, Nita Subject: Flinders Aluminum Fabrication Corp.	Agency: Bureau of Fire File: 6374 Investigator: Olsen Charge: NC 20-305 Report Date: December 1, 2007 Examination by: Victoria Faris Senior Criminalist

At the request of Chief Fire Marshal Olsen, clothing samples were examined for the presence of hydrochloric acid, iron filings, and shampoo. The clothing samples were reportedly from the deceased, George Avery, and were forwarded to the Crime Laboratory by the Office of the Medical Examiner on November 17, 2007. Returned to Olsen on December 1, 2007.

LABORATORY EXAMINATION

The following items were received:
Item 1 a blue plaid shirt with burnt sleeves;
Item 2 blue jeans;
Item 3 white briefs;
Item 4 white crew socks;
Item 5 a pair of white Nike athletic shoes

The clothing items were visually examined for particles, for stains indicative of acid exposure, and for shampoo residue. Stains on the blue jeans were tested for acidity (pH) and examined with x-ray fluorescence spectrometry (XRF) and chemical spot tests. Particulate debris from the blue jeans was examined with x-ray fluorescence spectrometry (XRF). A solid residue from the plaid shirt collar was tested for surfactant (sudsing) properties. Aqueous extracts of the soles of the Nike shoes were tested for pH and examined with x-ray fluorescence spectrometry (XRF) and chemical spot tests. The lower part of the sleeves of the shirt were burnt away and could not be examined for pH.

EXAMINATION CONCLUSIONS AND OBSERVATIONS

No indications of hydrochloric acid, such as acidity or chloride, were found in the blue jeans or the soles of the Nike shoes. This does not mean the items were not exposed to hydrochloric acid under circumstances in which it did not survive on the clothing, such as dilution or exposure to heat. A variety of metallic particles were found on the blue jeans, including aluminum, iron, and some with a composition of iron, nickel, and chromium, which are found in stainless steel. The solid residue from the left shirt collar exhibited sudsing properties when mixed with water, as would be expected from shampoo or soap products. No other tests were performed on the solid residue. This laboratory cannot determine the brand of shampoo.

Exhibit 24

Report of David Pinkus

RE: FIRE AT FLINDERS ALUMINUM FABRICATION CORPORATION'S
INDUSTRIAL PLANT, 187 RIVER ROAD, NITA CITY

DATE OF FIRE: November 16, 2007   **DATE OF REPORT:** May 1, 2008

I have thoroughly reviewed the report of Chief Fire Marshal Olsen. My analysis of the facts in his report leads me to conclude that the fire must be technically listed as an accident.

Hydrochloric acid is normally present at the plant because it is used to clean the aluminum products. Since it is stored in one place, this would explain the large quantity of hydrochloric acid at the point of origin of the fire. Chief Olsen's conclusion that hundreds of gallons were splashed about the room is pure conjecture based not on physical evidence, but upon the size of the fire. The explosion itself could explain the searing of the concrete and the presence of HCl in the debris. Given the elapsed time between ignition and observation, no conclusion as to the amount of acid involved or whether it was spread about is possible.

The smoke and flame of the fire were not observed until the fire was burning for one half hour. By this time, the building was being consumed by the fire. At this point, the color of the smoke and flame is affected by the burning building and not the acid.

In my opinion the rapid spread of the fire could have been caused by several factors. First, from my previous visits to the plant during fire prevention duties, the rooms were large, with considerable fuel loading, open, and provided favorable ventilation conditions that would encourage the fire to spread. Although the remaining structure showed that a window was open, there is no way of knowing if the other windows were open or closed, because most of the structure was destroyed. Second, since the building was very old, it was not constructed to prevent fire travel nor was it constructed to prevent many causes of accidental fires. Third, an accidental explosion involving fifty gallons of hydrochloric acid would result in the conflagration described in Chief Olsen's report. Fourth, accidental explosion would account for the fatality. It is unlikely that a professional arsonist would be so careless as to be caught in a fire of his own making.

Chief Olsen has not ruled out, nor could he, the possibility that a leak in a storage drum holding HCl could have resulted in the introduction of the acid throughout the storage room. If the acid came into contact with hot ferrous metal from any cause, an explosion could result.

The sheer magnitude of the physical destruction caused by the explosion, fire, and the volume of water poured on the fire would have washed away evidence of accidental causes such as faulty wiring, cigarette butts, and the like.

In arson investigation, no finding of arson should be made until all possible accidental causes are ruled out. Since accidental causes of the fire have not been satisfactorily eliminated, I am unable to conclude that the fire was the result of arson. As to the presence of Mr. Avery, I agree with Chief Olsen that his background should be gone into in some detail. Some of that background is disquieting. However, there is insufficient evidence to establish that Avery is an arsonist. Moreover, there is little evidence in this case, other than circumstances, to link him to the fire.

Submitted by:

David Pinkus

David Pinkus

Exhibit 25

Pinkus Curriculum Vitae

DAVID G. PINKUS

CURRICULUM VITAE

1975-1979   *United States Navy*

Officer Candidate School

Service, Manila, Philippines; Guam

While in service, assigned various combat and noncombat duties. Received specialized training in fighting on-ship fires, including aircraft carriers, destroyers, and patrol craft. Was assigned supervisory responsibility for on-board fire fighting teams. Achieved rank of lieutenant.

1980-1984   Firefighter, Fire Investigator, Nita City Fire Department

Attended Fireman Training Academy, Nita City, followed by two years service as a firefighter for the Fire Department. Involved in multiple fire-fighting operations, including residential and commercial structures and involving multiple mechanisms of fire initiation.

Joined the National Fire Emergency Rescue team and engaged in forest fire-fighting operations in Colorado, Idaho, and Yellowstone National Park.

Accepted for intensive training in arson investigation offered by Colorado College, followed by two years service as an arson investigator in the Nita City Bureau of Fire Investigation.

1984-2003   Deputy Fire Marshal, Nita City Bureau of Fire Investigation

Appointed Deputy Fire Marshal in charge of arson investigation, and supervised an investigation team that grew from three investigators to twenty-nine investigators over the course of twenty years. Attended a series of six national seminars on aspects of arson investigation, including uses of accelerants, explosives, household compounds, and commonly available chemicals and ignition devices.

Have taught courses in arson investigation and investigative procedures at the Nita City Bureau of Fire Investigation and at the Nita Fire Department Training School in East Meadow.

Retired from the Bureau with commendation, February 6, 2003.

2003 to Present   Consultant and Lecturer in Arson Investigation Techniques

> For past six years, have worked as a forensic consultant in both civil and criminal cases involving unexplained fires and explosions. Have worked for both plaintiffs and defendants in civil cases and both the State and the defendant in criminal cases. Have lectured at a number of seminars on the subject of modernizing arson investigation techniques.

PROFESSIONAL ASSOCIATIONS AND ORGANIZATIONS

- Past president, Nita State Association of Fire Fighters
- National Board Member, National Association of Fire Fighters
- Member, Joint Task Force Nita City/County Arson Investigation Modernization
- Member and Past Vice President, National Emergency Response Team

PUBLICATIONS

National Association of Fire Fighters Newsletter, "Short Fuse Ignition Devices in Intentionally Set Fires," Vol. 4: 28–32 (1996)

Chapter, "Modern Techniques for Site Recovery of Accelerant Residue," in *Arson Investigation*, Houghton Miflin (2003)

Memorandum Re: Pinkus

MEMORANDUM

TO: Counsel for Mismo Fire Insurance

FROM: Legal Assistant

RE: David Pinkus

At your request, I have checked with several attorneys about Plaintiff's fire expert in the Flinders case, David Pinkus.

Mr. Pinkus is known more by criminal attorneys for his opinions in alleged arson cases. He is thought of as fair minded and balanced in his approach. Both the prosecution and defense have retained him in such cases, as stated in his resume. In the civil arena, Mr. Pinkus has been retained primarily (somewhere in the neighborhood of 90 percent of the time, from what I can tell) by members of the plaintiff's bar to refute charges of arson leveled by insurance companies when denying damage claims due to fire. Nobody I talked to remembers him ever testifying in civil court that a fire was purposefully set. Rather, he usually attacks the findings of the investigation team.

Based on counsel's 26(a)(2)(B) disclosure, he is paid $300 an hour for consulting work and report writing, $3,000 a day (and $2,000 for half a day) when testifying at deposition or in court, and has thus far billed $3,000 in this case for phone calls, meetings, review of material, and writing his report.

EXHIBIT 26

Video of Flinders Fire (on CD)

Exhibit 27

Video of Yaphank Fire (on CD)

Exhibit 28

Anderson Bank Memo

First Trust Bank
Nita City, Nita 12305

MEMORANDUM

TO: Gerald Laughlin
Loan Review Committee,

FROM: John Anderson, Vice President

DATE: October 15, 2007

RE: Flinders Transition Plan

I have had several meetings this month with Arthur Jackson, President of Flinders Aluminum, in which he has requested new financing and an adjustment of current financing with the bank. I have reviewed the proposed concept of transitioning the Flinders Aluminum plant that currently manufactures siding for housing to an autoparts manufacturing plant and am seeking additional information from our client in this regard. Given the admitted recent earnings track record at Flinders, the time has come for such a transition and, if handled deftly, this could be a very promising investment. I have asked the client to provide financial data, market studies, tax returns, and product designs (surprisingly, none have been provided to date), which, if they pan out, will encourage our participation. The land value alone in this riverfront area could provide the requisite security for any investment.

I will advise when the follow-up information arrives.

JURY INSTRUCTIONS

Preliminary Instruction 1 – Introduction

You have been selected as jurors and have taken an oath to well and truly try this cause. This trial will last one day. During the progress of the trial there will be periods of time when the Court recesses. During those periods of time, you must not talk about this case among yourselves or with anyone else.

During the trial, do not talk to any of the parties, their lawyers, or any of the witnesses. If any attempt is made by anyone to talk to you concerning the matters here under consideration, you should immediately report that fact to the Court.

You should keep an open mind. You should not form or express an opinion during the trial and should reach no conclusion in this case until you have heard all of the evidence, the arguments of counsel, and the final instructions as to the law that will be given to you by the Court.

Preliminary Instruction 2 – Conduct of the Trial

First, the attorneys will have an opportunity to make opening statements. These statements are not evidence and should be considered only as a preview of what the attorneys expect the evidence will be.

Following the opening statements, witnesses will be called to testify. They will be placed under oath and questioned by the attorneys. Documents and other tangible exhibits may also be received as evidence. If an exhibit is given to you to examine, you should examine it carefully, individually, and without any comment.

It is counsel's right and duty to object when testimony or other evidence is being offered that he or she believes is not admissible. When the Court sustains an objection to a question, the jurors must disregard the question and the answer, if one has been given, and draw no inference from the question or answer or speculate as to what the witness would have said if permitted to answer. Jurors must also disregard evidence stricken from the record.

When the Court sustains an objection to any evidence, the jurors must disregard that evidence. When the Court overrules an objection to any evidence, the jurors must not give that evidence any more weight than if the objection had not been made.

When the evidence is completed, the attorneys will make final statements. These final statements are not evidence but are given to assist you in evaluating the evidence. The attorneys are also permitted to argue in an attempt to persuade you to a particular verdict. You may accept or reject those arguments as you see fit.

Finally, just before you retire to consider your verdict, I will give you further instructions on the law that applies to this case.

Final Instructions

Members of the jury, the evidence in this case has been completed, and I will now instruct you as to the law.

The law applicable to this case is stated in these instructions, and it is your duty to follow all of them. You must not single out certain instructions and disregard others.

It is your duty to determine the facts, and to determine them only from the evidence in this case. You are to apply the law to the facts and in this way decide the case. You must not be governed or influenced by sympathy or prejudice for or against any party in this case. Your verdict must be based on evidence and not upon speculation, guess, or conjecture.

From time to time the court has ruled on the admissibility of evidence. You must not concern yourselves with the reasons for these rulings. You should disregard questions and exhibits that were withdrawn or to which objections were sustained.

You should also disregard testimony and exhibits that the court has refused or stricken.

The evidence that you should consider consists only of the witnesses' testimonies and the exhibits the court has received.

Any evidence that was received for a limited purpose should not be considered by you for any other purpose.

You should consider all the evidence in the light of your own observations and experiences in life.

Neither by these instructions nor by any ruling or remark that I have made do I mean to indicate any opinion as to the facts or as to what your verdict should be.

1. Opening statements are made by the attorneys to acquaint you with the facts they expect to prove. Closing arguments are made by the attorneys to discuss the facts and circumstances in the case, and should be confined to the evidence and to reasonable inferences to be drawn therefrom. Neither opening statements nor closing arguments are evidence, and any statement or argument made by the attorneys that is not based on the evidence should be disregarded.

2. You are the sole judges of the credibility of the witnesses and of the weight to be given to the testimony of each witness. In determining what credit is to be given any witness, you may take into account his or her ability and opportunity to observe; his or her manner and appearance while testifying; any interest, bias, or prejudice he or she may have; the reasonableness of the testimony considered in the light of all the evidence; and any other factors that bear on the believability and weight of the witness's testimony.

3. You have heard evidence in this case from witnesses who testified as experts. The law allows experts to express an opinion on subjects involving their special knowledge, training and skill, experience, or research. While their opinions are allowed to be given, it is entirely within the province of the jury to determine what weight shall be given their testimony. Jurors are not bound by the testimony of experts; their testimony is to be weighed as that of any other witness.

4. The law recognizes two kinds of evidence: direct and circumstantial. Direct evidence proves a fact directly; that is, the evidence by itself, if true, establishes the fact. Circumstantial evidence is the proof of facts or circumstances that give rise to a reasonable inference of other facts; that is, circumstantial evidence proves a fact indirectly in that it follows from other facts or circumstances according to common experience and observations in life. An eyewitness is a common example of direct evidence, while human footprints are circumstantial evidence that a person was present.

The law makes no distinction between direct and circumstantial evidence as to the degree or amount of proof required, and each should be considered according to whatever weight or value it may have. All of the evidence should be considered and evaluated by you in arriving at your verdict.

5. The information in this case is the formal method of accusing the defendant of a crime and placing him on trial. It is not any evidence against the defendant and does not create any inference of guilt. The State has the burden of proving beyond a reasonable doubt every essential element of the crime charged in the information or any of the crimes included therein.

6. The State has the burden of proving the guilt of the defendant beyond a reasonable doubt, and this burden remains on the State throughout the case. The defendant is not required to prove his innocence.

7. Reasonable doubt means a doubt based upon reason and common sense that arises from a fair and rational consideration of all the evidence or lack of evidence in the case. It is a doubt that is not a vague, speculative, or imaginary doubt, but such a doubt as would cause reasonable persons to hesitate to act in matters of importance to themselves.

8. The defendant is presumed to be innocent of the charges against him. This presumption remains with him throughout every stage of the trial and during your deliberations on the verdict. The presumption is not overcome until, from all the evidence in the case, you are convinced beyond a reasonable doubt that the defendant is guilty.

IN THE CIRCUIT COURT OF
DARROW COUNTY, STATE OF NITA
CRIMINAL DIVISION

THE STATE OF NITA,

vs.   CASE NO. CR-70410-1

ARTHUR JACKSON,
  Defendant.

COMMERCIAL ARSON

We, the jury, find the Defendant, Arthur Jackson, NOT GUILTY.

_____

    Foreperson

We, the jury, find the Defendant, Arthur Jackson, GUILTY.

_____

    Foreperson

Special Impeachment Problems

Problem 1: Marie Williams

Assume that Ms. Williams has testified at trial on direct examination that she was never bitter or angry at Mr. Jackson, and she just wanted the best for him when their relationship terminated.

(a) For the Defense, conduct a cross-examination and impeachment of Ms. Williams.

(b) For the State, conduct a redirect examination to the extent necessary to rehabilitate.

Problem 2: Marie Williams

Assume that Ms. Williams has testified at trial on direct examination that when she confronted Mr. Jackson with her suspicions that he had hired an arsonist, Mr. Jackson looked away from her and said, "Marie, you know the trouble I'm in." Assume further that Ms. Williams testified on direct that she went to the police "immediately" after this conversation with Mr. Jackson.

(a) For the Defense, conduct a cross-examination and impeachment of Ms. Williams.

(b) For the State, conduct a redirect examination to the extent necessary to rehabilitate.

Problem 3: John Anderson

Assume that Mr. Anderson has testified at trial on direct examination that when he asked Mr. Jackson for financial information on the company, Mr. Jackson said the information had already been compiled and would be brought to the bank the next day. Assume further that Mr. Anderson testified on direct that he asked Mr. Jackson for additional collateral for the loan, but Mr. Jackson said he had no additional collateral available, that he was "tapped out."

(a) For the Defense, conduct a cross-examination and impeachment of Mr. Anderson.

(b) For the State, conduct a redirect examination to the extent necessary to rehabilitate.

PROBLEM 4: ARTHUR JACKSON

Assume that Mr. Jackson has testified at trial on direct examination that he hired Mr. Avery based upon Ms. Peterson's recommendation and after he had called Yaphank and Fass to verify Mr. Avery's achievements.

(a) For the State, conduct a cross-examination and impeachment of Mr. Jackson.

(b) For the Defense, conduct a redirect examination to the extent necessary to rehabilitate.

PROBLEM 5: ARTHUR JACKSON

Assume that Mr. Jackson has testified at trial on direct examination that he never saw or spoke to George Avery on the night of the fire, and that he saw Marie Williams as he was leaving around 6:30 p.m.

(a) For the State, conduct a cross-examination and impeachment of Mr. Jackson.

(b) For the Defense, conduct a redirect examination to the extent necessary to rehabilitate.

PROBLEM 6: ARTHUR JACKSON

Assume that Mr. Jackson has testified at trial on direct examination that at the time of the fire he was already in the process of compiling the documents the bank wanted and that he had already contacted General Motors about the plans.

(a) For the State, conduct a cross-examination and impeachment of Mr. Jackson.

(b) For the Defense, conduct a redirect examination to the extent necessary to rehabilitate.

PROBLEM 7: SONIA PETERSON

Assume that Ms. Peterson has testified at trial on direct examination that both she and Mr. Jackson checked on Mr. Avery's credentials and resume before he was hired at Flinders.

(a) For the State, conduct a cross-examination and impeachment of Mr. Jackson.

(b) For the Defense, conduct a redirect examination to the extent necessary to rehabilitate.

Black Slide   **Slide 1**

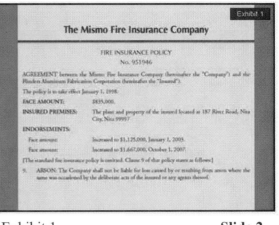

Exhibit 1   **Slide 2**

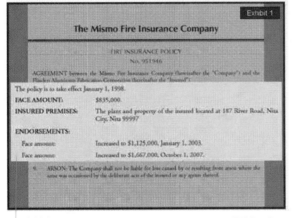

Exhibit 1   **Slide 3**

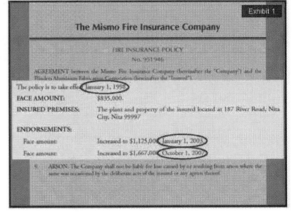

Exhibit 1   **Slide 4**

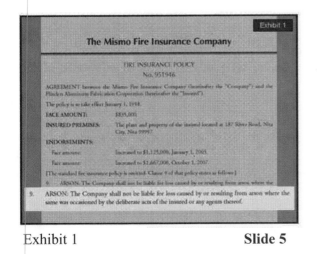

Exhibit 1   **Slide 5**

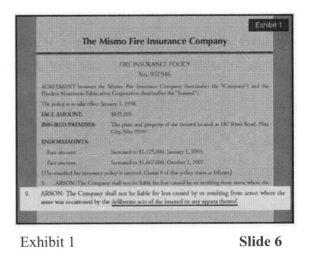

Exhibit 1   **Slide 6**

Exhibit 2   **Slide 7**

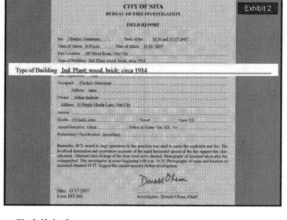

Exhibit 2   **Slide 8**

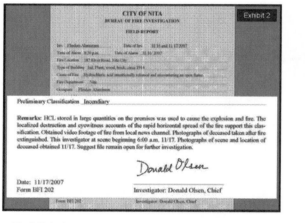

Exhibit 2   **Slide 9**

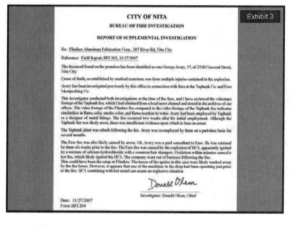

Exhibit 3   **Slide 10**

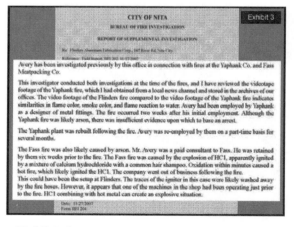

Exhibit 3   **Slide 11**

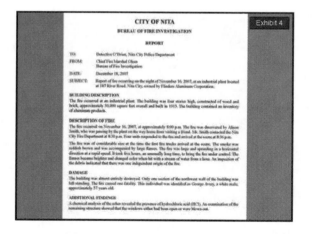

Exhibit 4, p.1   **Slide 12**

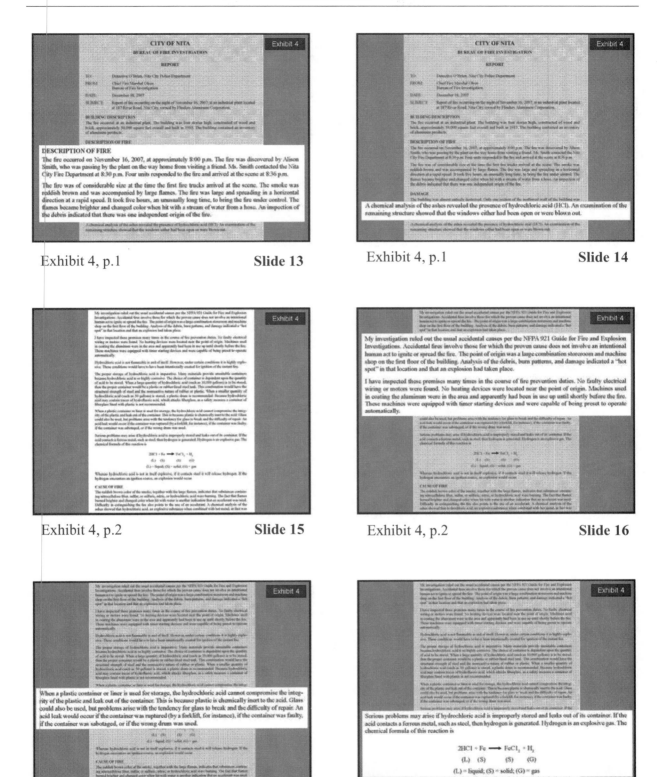

Exhibit 4, p.1   **Slide 13**

Exhibit 4, p.1   **Slide 14**

Exhibit 4, p.2   **Slide 15**

Exhibit 4, p.2   **Slide 16**

Exhibit 4, p.2   **Slide 17**

Exhibit 4, p.2   **Slide 18**

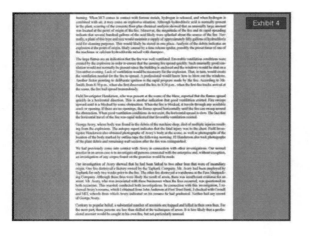

Exhibit 4, p.3   **Slide 19**

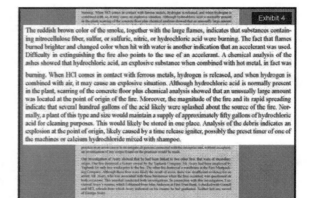

The reddish brown color of the smoke, together with the large flames, indicates that substances containing nitrocellulose fiber, sulfur, or sulfuric, nitric, or hydrochloric acid were burning. The fact that flames burned brighter and changed color when hit with water is another indication that an accelerant was used. Difficulty in extinguishing the fire also points to the use of an accelerant. A chemical analysis of the ashes showed that hydrochloric acid, an explosive substance when combined with hot metal, in fact was burning. When HCl comes in contact with ferrous metals, hydrogen is released, and when hydrogen is combined with air, it may cause an explosive situation. Although hydrochloric acid is normally present in the plant, scarring of the concrete floor plus chemical analysis showed that an unusually large amount was located at the point of origin of the fire. Moreover, the magnitude of the fire and its rapid spreading indicate that several hundred gallons of the acid likely were splashed about the source of the fire. Normally, a plant of this type and size would maintain a supply of approximately fifty gallons of hydrochloric acid for cleaning purposes. This would likely be stored in one place. Analysis of the debris indicates an explosion at the point of origin, likely caused by a time release igniter, possibly the preset timer of one of the machines or calcium hydrochloride mixed with shampoo.

Exhibit 4, p.3   **Slide 20**

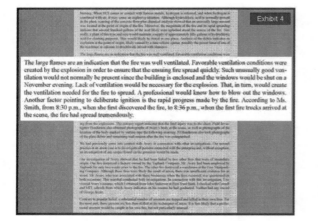

The large flames are an indication that the fire was well ventilated. Favorable ventilation conditions were created by the explosion in order to ensure that the ensuing fire spread quickly. Such unusually good ventilation would not normally be present since the building is enclosed and the windows would be shut on a November evening. Lack of ventilation would be necessary for the explosion. That, in turn, would create the ventilation needed for the fire to spread. A professional would know how to blow out the windows. Another factor pointing to deliberate ignition is the rapid progress made by the fire. According to Ms. Smith, from 8:30 p.m., when she first discovered the fire, to 8:36 p.m., when the first fire trucks arrived at the scene, the fire had spread tremendously.

Exhibit 4, p.3   **Slide 21**

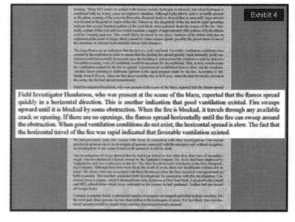

Field Investigator Henderson, who was present at the scene of the blaze, reported that the flames spread quickly in a horizontal direction. This is another indication that good ventilation existed. Fire sweeps upward until it is blocked by some obstruction. When the fire is blocked, it travels through any available crack or opening. If there are no openings, the flames spread horizontally until the fire can sweep around the obstruction. When good ventilation conditions do not exist, the horizontal spread is slow. The fact that the horizontal travel of the fire was rapid indicated that favorable ventilation existed.

Exhibit 4, p.3   **Slide 22**

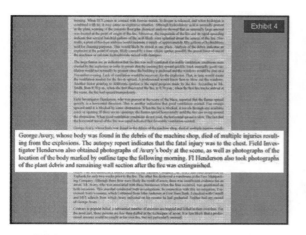

George Avery, whose body was found in the debris of the machine shop, died of multiple injuries resulting from the explosions. The autopsy report indicates that the fatal injury was to the chest. Field Investigator Henderson also obtained photographs of Avery's body at the scene, as well as photographs of the location of the body marked by outline tape the following morning. FI Henderson also took photographs of the plant debris and remaining wall section after the fire was extinguished.

Exhibit 4, p.3   **Slide 23**

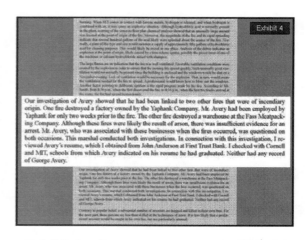

Our investigation of Avery showed that he had been linked to two other fires that were of incendiary origin. One fire destroyed a factory owned by the Yaphank Company. Mr. Avery had been employed by Yaphank for only two weeks prior to the fire. The other fire destroyed a warehouse at the Fass Meatpacking Company. Although these fires were likely the result of arson, there was insufficient evidence for an arrest. Mr. Avery, who was associated with these businesses when the fires occurred, was questioned on both occasions. This marshal conducted both investigations. In connection with this investigation, I reviewed Avery's resume, which I obtained from John Anderson at First Trust Bank. I checked with Cornell and MIT, schools from which Avery indicated on his resume he had graduated. Neither had any record of George Avery.

Exhibit 4, p.3   **Slide 24**

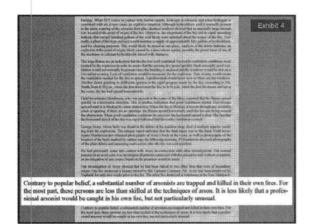

Exhibit 4, p.3 **Slide 25**

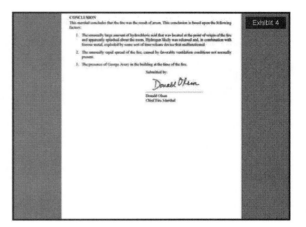

Exhibit 4, p.4 **Slide 26**

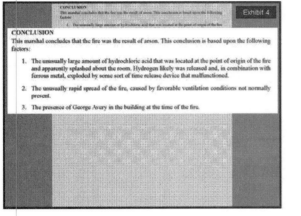

Exhibit 4, p.4 **Slide 27**

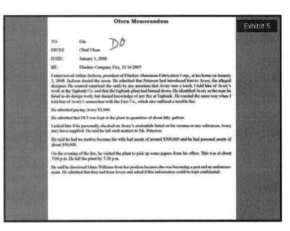

Exhibit 5 **Slide 28**

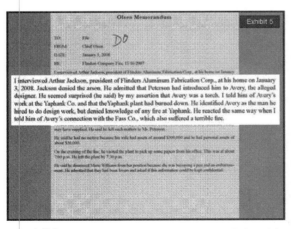

Exhibit 5 **Slide 29**

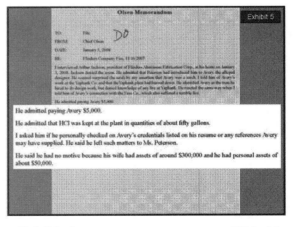

Exhibit 5 **Slide 30**

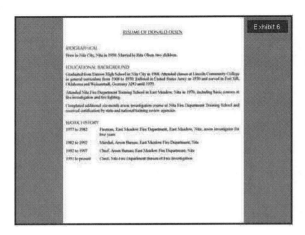

Exhibit 6   **Slide 31**

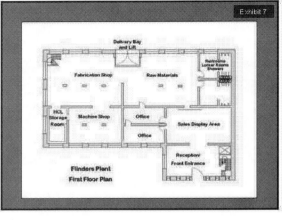

Exhibit 7   **Slide 32**

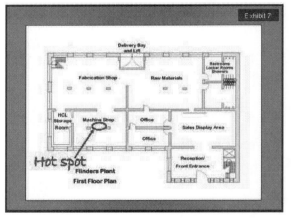

Exhibit 7   **Slide 33**

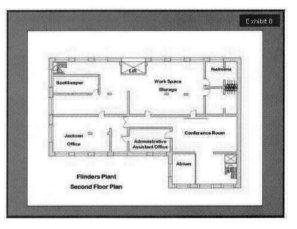

Exhibit 8   **Slide 34**

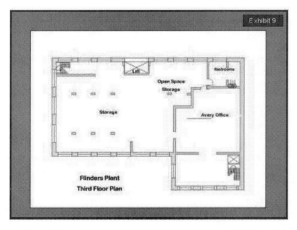

Exhibit 9   **Slide 35**

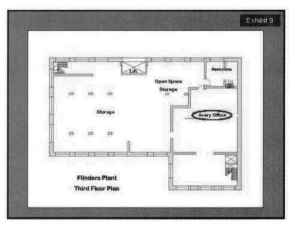

Exhibit 9   **Slide 36**

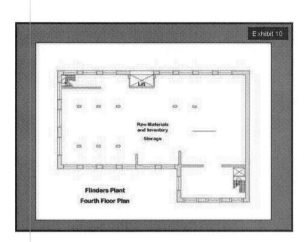

Exhibit 10   **Slide 37**

Exhibit 11   **Slide 38**

Exhibit 12   **Slide 39**

Exhibit 13   **Slide 40**

Exhibit 14   **Slide 41**

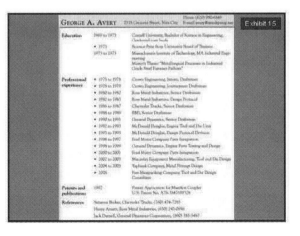

Exhibit 15   **Slide 42**

Exhibit 15

Slide 43

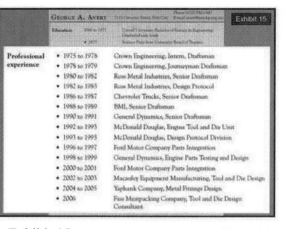

Exhibit 15

Slide 44

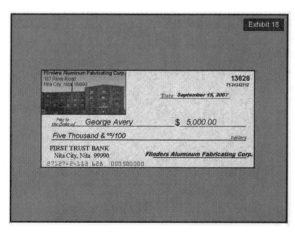

Exhibit 16

Slide 45

Exhibit 17

Slide 46

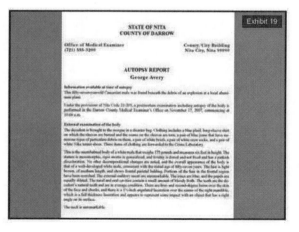

Exhibit 18

Slide 47

Exhibit 19, p.1

Slide 48

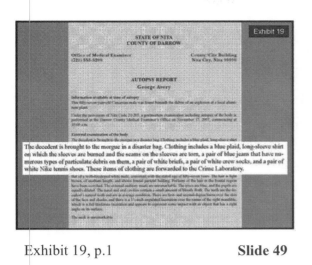

Exhibit 19, p.1   **Slide 49**

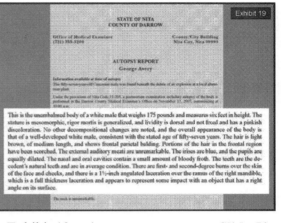

Exhibit 19, p.1   **Slide 50**

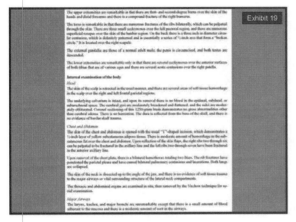

Exhibit 19, p.2   **Slide 51**

Exhibit 19, p.2   **Slide 52**

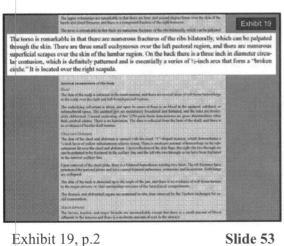

Exhibit 19, p.2   **Slide 53**

Exhibit 19, p.2   **Slide 54**

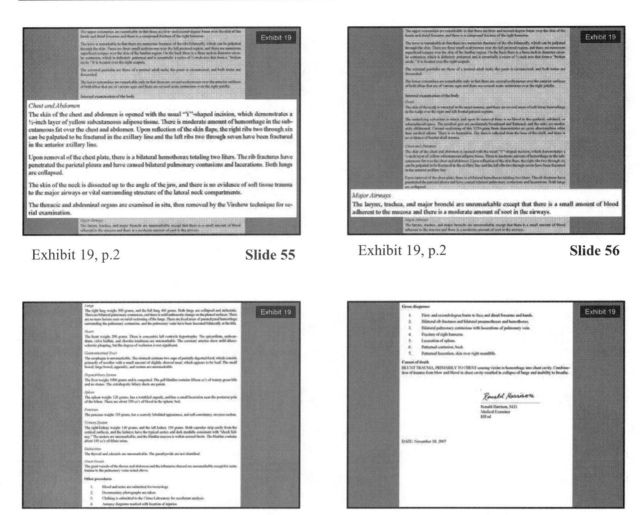

Exhibit 19, p.2   **Slide 55**

Exhibit 19, p.2   **Slide 56**

Exhibit 19, p.3   **Slide 57**

Exhibit 19, p.4   **Slide 58**

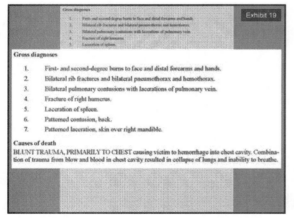

Exhibit 19, p.4   **Slide 59**

Gross diagnoses

1. First- and second-degree burns to face and distal forearms and hands.
2. Bilateral rib fractures and bilateral pneumothorax and hemothorax.
3. Bilateral pulmonary contusions with lacerations of pulmonary vein.
4. Fracture of right humerus.
5. Laceration of spleen.
6. Patterned contusion, back.
7. Patterned laceration, skin over right mandible.

Causes of death

BLUNT TRAUMA, PRIMARILY TO CHEST causing victim to hemorrhage into chest cavity. Combination of trauma from blow and blood in chest cavity resulted in collapse of lungs and inability to breathe.

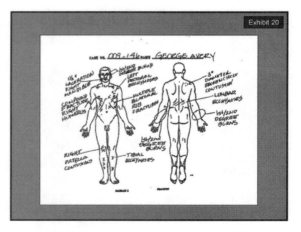

Exhibit 20   **Slide 60**

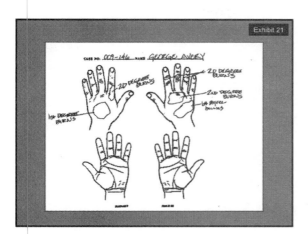

Exhibit 21   **Slide 61**

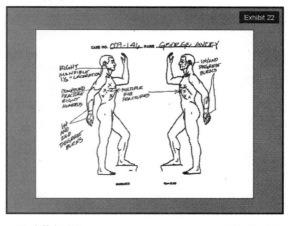

Exhibit 22   **Slide 62**

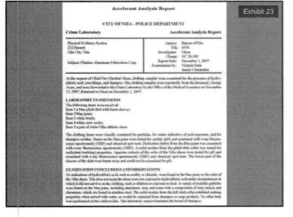

Exhibit 23   **Slide 63**

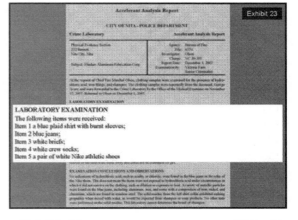

Exhibit 23   **Slide 64**

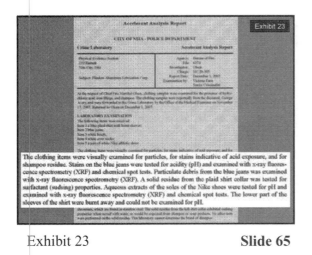

Exhibit 23   **Slide 65**

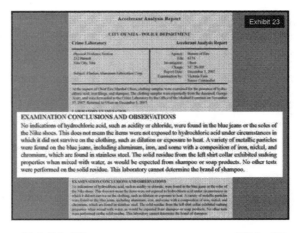

Exhibit 23   **Slide 66**

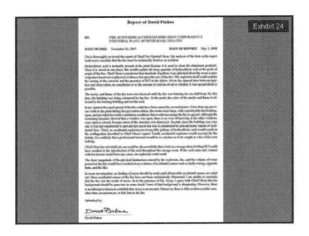

Exhibit 24   **Slide 67**

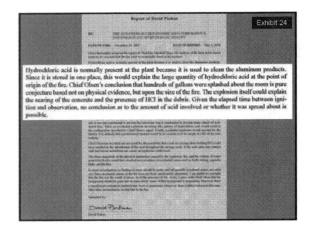

Exhibit 24   **Slide 68**

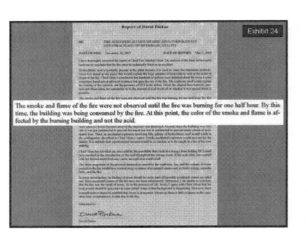

Exhibit 24   **Slide 69**

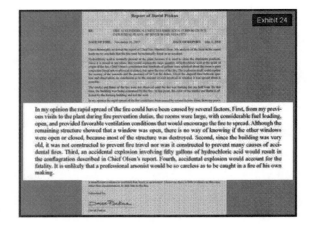

Exhibit 24   **Slide 70**

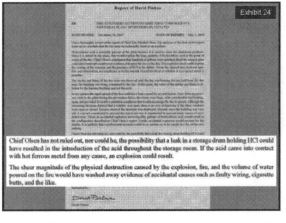

Exhibit 24   **Slide 71**

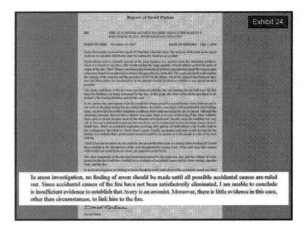

Exhibit 24   **Slide 72**

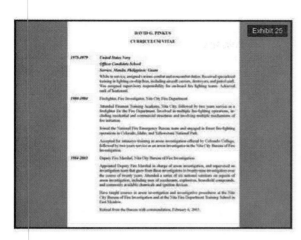

Exhibit 25, p.1 **Slide 73**

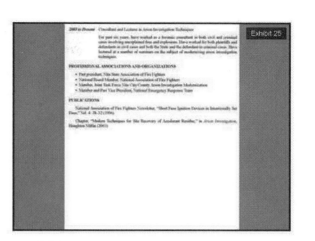

Exhibit 25, p.2 **Slide 74**

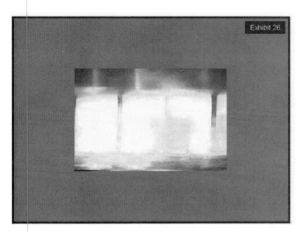

Exhibit 26 **Slide 75**

Exhibit 27 **Slide 76**

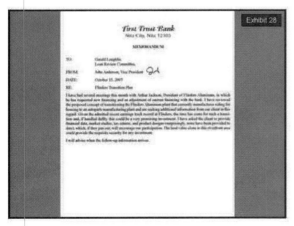

Exhibit 28 **Slide 77**

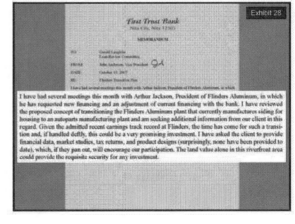

Exhibit 28 **Slide 78**

Information   **Slide 79**

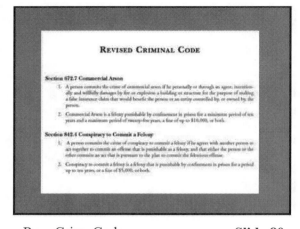

Rev. Crim. Code   **Slide 80**

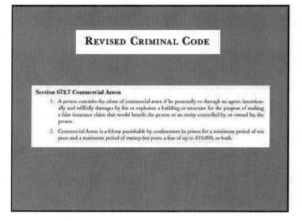

Arson 672.7   **Slide 81**

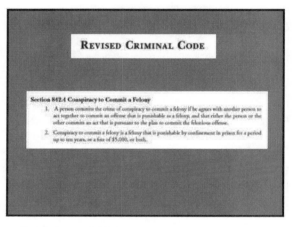

Conspiracy 842.4   **Slide 82**

Interview Notes   **Slide 83**

Plea Ag., p.1   **Slide 84**

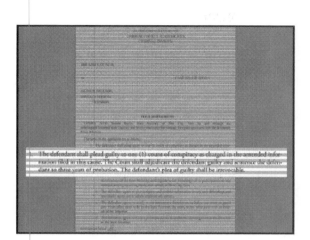

Plea Ag., p.1   **Slide 85**

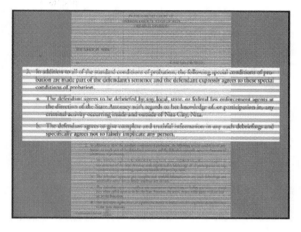

Plea Ag., p.1   **Slide 86**

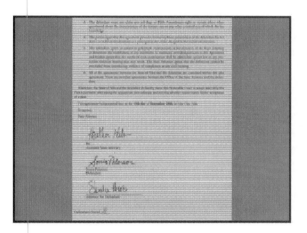

Plea Ag., p.2   **Slide 87**

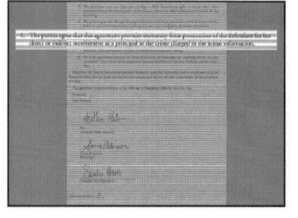

Plea Ag., p.2   **Slide 88**

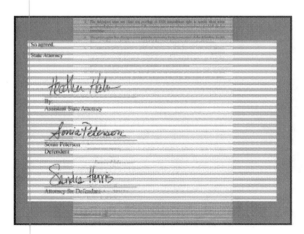

Plea Ag., p.2   **Slide 89**

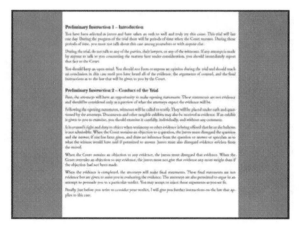

J I Prelim.   **Slide 90**

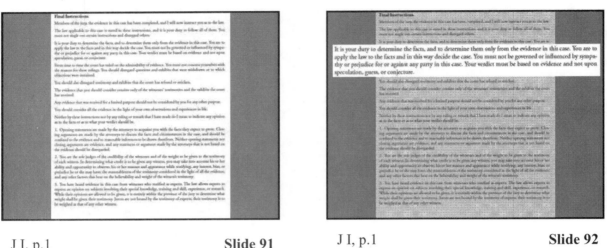

J I, p.1　　　　　　　　　　**Slide 91**

J I, p.1　　　　　　　　　　**Slide 92**

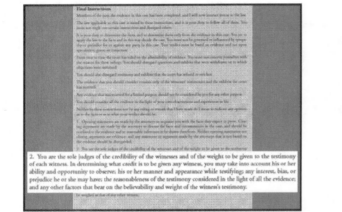

J I, p.1　　　　　　　　　　**Slide 93**

J I, p.1　　　　　　　　　　**Slide 94**

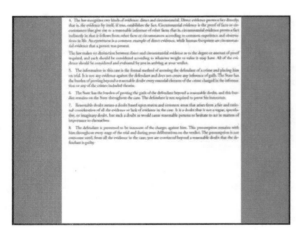

J I, p.2　　　　　　　　　　**Slide 95**

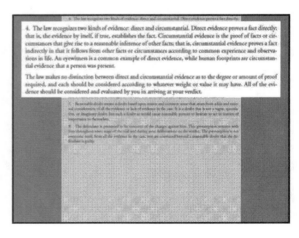

J I, p.2　　　　　　　　　　**Slide 96**

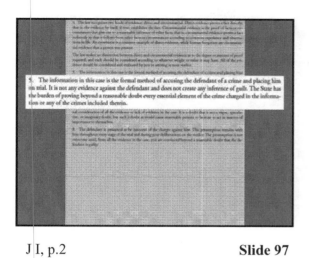

J I, p.2   **Slide 97**

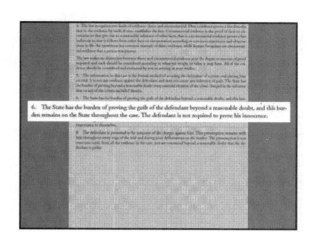

J I, p.2   **Slide 98**

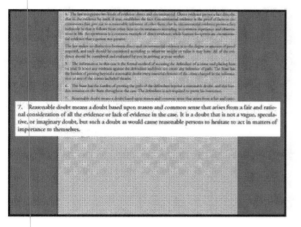

J I, p.2   **Slide 99**

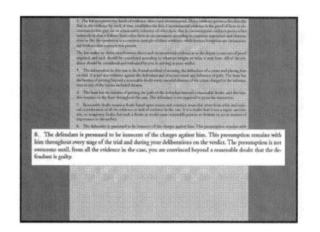

J I, p.2   **Slide 100**

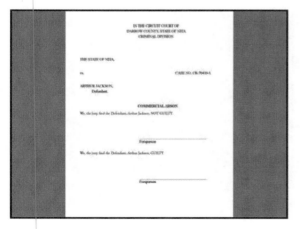

Verdict Form   **Slide 101**

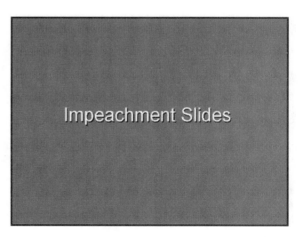

Impeachment Slides   **Slide 102**

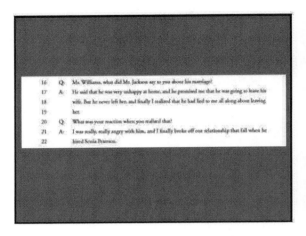

MW, p. 7, L 16–22   **Slide 103**

MW, p. 7, L 16–22   **Slide 104**

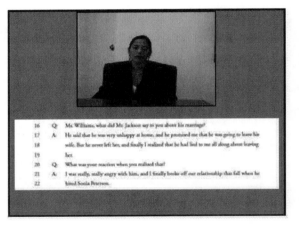

MW, p. 7, L 16–22 video +   **Slide 105**

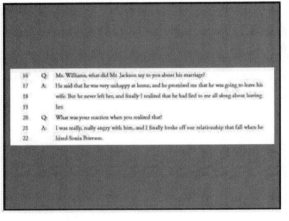

MW, p. 7, L 16–22 reveal   **Slide 106**

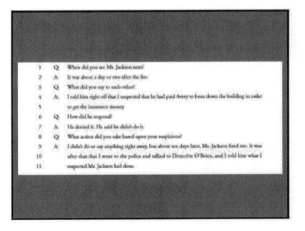

MW, p. 8, L 1–11   **Slide 107**

MW, p. 8, L 1–11 video   **Slide 108**

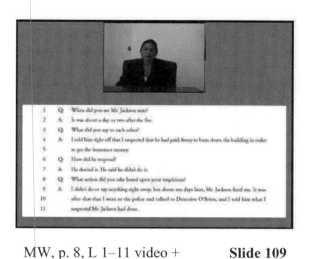

MW, p. 8, L 1–11 video +   **Slide 109**

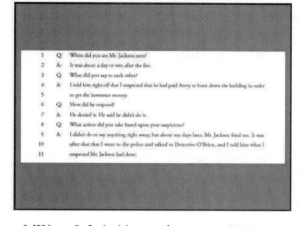

MW, p. 8, L 1–11 reveal   **Slide 110**

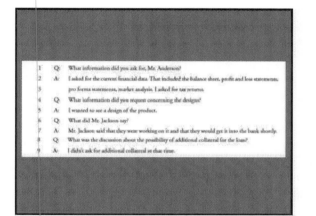

JA, p.11–12, L1–9   **Slide 111**

JA, p.11–12, L1–9 video   **Slide 112**

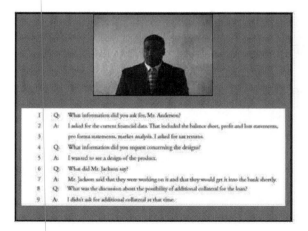

JA, p.11–12, L1–9 video +   **Slide 113**

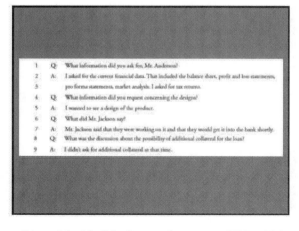

JA, p.11–12, L1–9 reveal   **Slide 114**

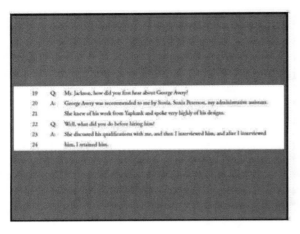

AJ, p. 13, L19–24   **Slide 115**

AJ, p. 13, L19–24 video   **Slide 116**

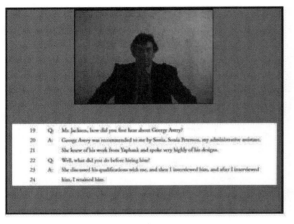

AJ, p. 13, L19–24 video +   **Slide 117**

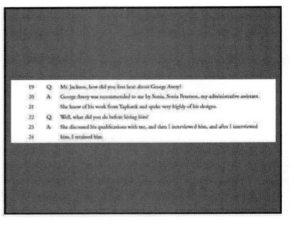

AJ, p. 13, L19–24 reveal   **Slide 118**

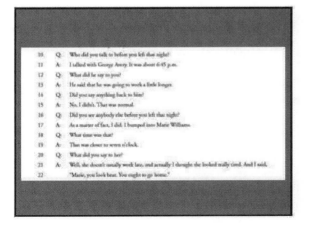

AJ, p. 14, L10–22   **Slide 119**

AJ, p. 14, L10–22 video   **Slide 120**

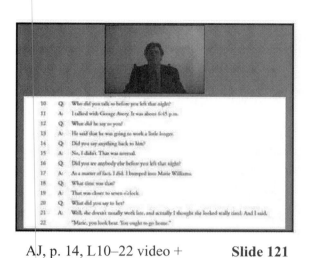

AJ, p. 14, L10–22 video +   **Slide 121**

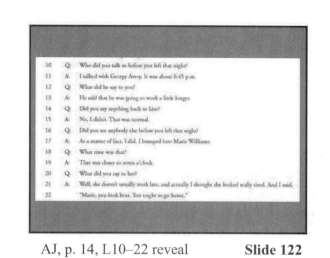

AJ, p. 14, L10–22 reveal   **Slide 122**

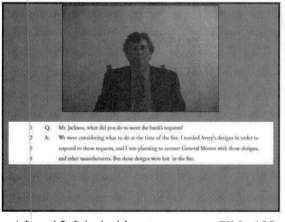

AJ, p. 15, L1–4   **Slide 123**

AJ, p. 15, L1–4 video   **Slide 124**

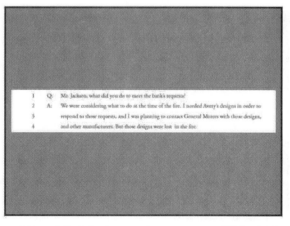

AJ, p. 15, L1–4 video +   **Slide 125**

AJ, p. 15, L1–4 reveal   **Slide 126**

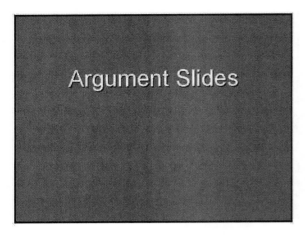

Argument Slides   **Slide 127**

Flinders Collapse - The Situation

2004-2006	*Aluminum siding market collapses*
2006	*Flinders loses $500,000*
2007	*Flinders loses $500,000 in first 9 months*
July 2007	*"If no new accounts, we're going under"*
July-Nov '07	*Jackson complains of financial problems*
Sept 2007	*Jackson hires Avery—Key & $5,000*
Sept 2007	*Jackson ups insurance $542,000*
Oct 2007	*Meets with Bank—loan dueNo $$ info—No plans—Bank refuses—No approval*
Nov 16, '07	*Fire destroys plant—Avery at point of origin*
Nov 28, '07	*$400,000 loan due—Never paid*

Animated   **Slide 128**

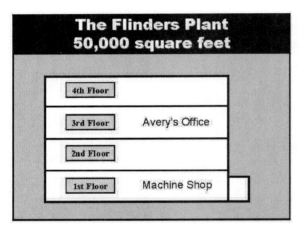

Slide 129

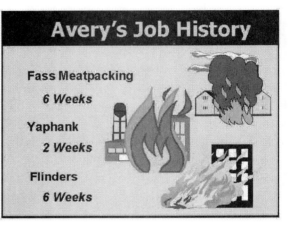

Animated   **Slide 130**

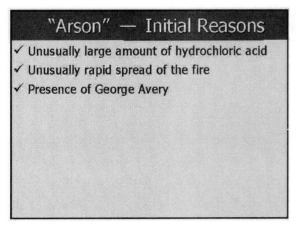

Animated   **Slide 131**

"Arson" — Final Reasons

- ✓ Unusually large amount of hydrochloric acid
- ✓ Unusually rapid spread of the fire
- ✓ Presence of George Avery
- ✓ Financial condition of the company
- ✓ Timing of increase in insurance
- ✓ Due date for $400,000 loan
- ✓ Avery is a stranger—No background check
- ✓ Bank says "No" —No plans, financials, studies
- ✓ Jackson lies about available funds

Animated   **Slide 132**

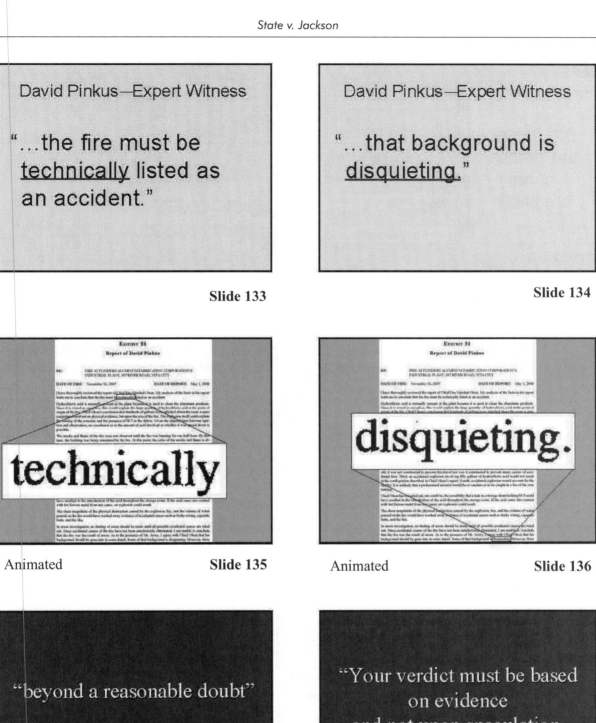

David Pinkus—Expert Witness

"...the fire must be <u>technically</u> listed as an accident."

Slide 133

David Pinkus—Expert Witness

"...that background is <u>disquieting.</u>"

Slide 134

Animated   **Slide 135**

Animated   **Slide 136**

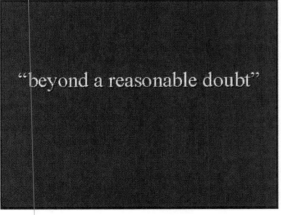

"beyond a reasonable doubt"

Slide 137

"Your verdict must be based on evidence and not upon speculation, guess or conjecture."

Slide 138

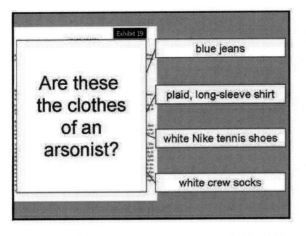

Animated   **Slide 139**

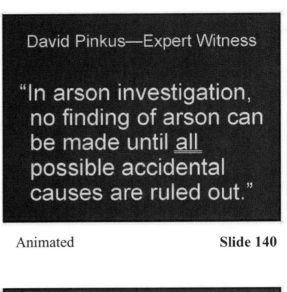

Animated   **Slide 140**

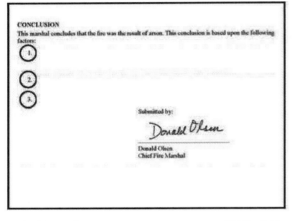

Animated   **Slide 141**

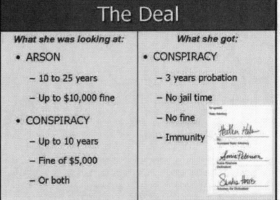

Animated   **Slide 142**

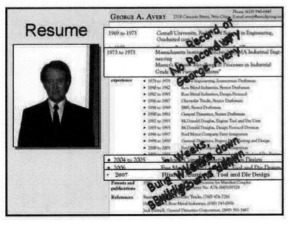

Animated   **Slide 143**

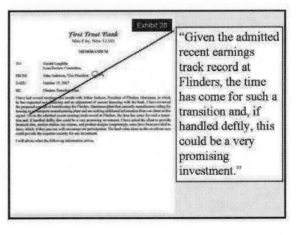

Animated   **Slide 144**

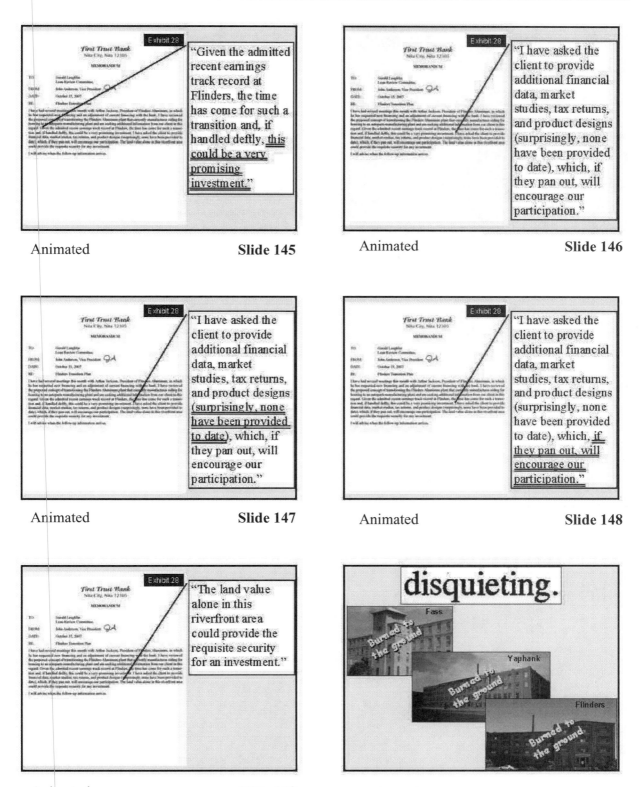

Animated   **Slide 145**

Animated   **Slide 146**

Animated   **Slide 147**

Animated   **Slide 148**

Animated   **Slide 149**

Animated   **Slide 150**

Donald Olsen

- 1977-82 Fireman, East Meadow Fire Department
  - Arson investigator for 2 years
- 1982-92 Marshal, Arson Bureau, East Meadow
- 1992-97 Chief, Arson Bureau, East Meadow
- 1997- Chief, Nita Fire Department
  Bureau of Fire Investigation
- Investigated Flinders fire
- Subpoenaed to testify

Animated   **Slide 151**

David Pinkus

- **1975-79** U.S. Navy, Fire fighting
  - Rank of Lieutenant
- **1980-84** Firefighter & Investigator, Nita Fire Dept.
- **1984-2003** Deputy Fire Marshall, Nita City Bureau
  - In charge of Arson Investigation
- **2003-** Forensic consultant, Lecturer
- **Past President, Nita Association of Fire Fighters**
- **Publications on Arson Investigation**

Animated   **Slide 152**

Chief Olsen	Mr. Pinkus
• Chief, Nita Fire Dept.	• Deputy under Olsen
• Chief, Arson Bureau	• Firefighter & investigator
• East Meadow	• Nita Fire Department
• Investigated Flinders	• Didn't
• Talked with witnesses	• Didn't
• Talked with firefighters	• Didn't
• Sifted through rubble	• Didn't
• Experienced with Avery	• Avery "disquieting"
• Subpoenaed, not hired	• Paid expert
• Conclusion: Arson	• "technically" not arson

Animated   **Slide 153**

The NITA Foundation

supports NITA's core values of excellence, ethics, mentoring, inclusiveness, justice, and philanthropy through our various programs. We strive to give back to our global community by supporting the work of attorneys engaged in the representation of the underserved, indigent, and disenfranchised. To learn more about NITA's publications, programs, or the work of our Foundation, please visit us online at www.nitafoundation.org or by calling (877) 648-2632.

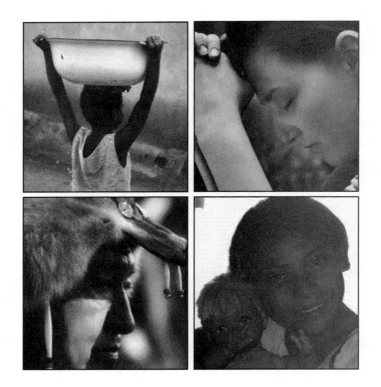

The NITA Foundation